I0494445

This colouring book for adults contains 50 of the best, most relaxing pictures for grownup who love to colour.

Each image has been carefully created, inspired by patterns that occur in nature, to ensure your colouring experience is the best it can be.

If you are stressed and struggling to relax in this busy, crazy world we live in, then the images in this book will give you the well-earned rest you deserve

Sometimes when we are stressed we cannot focus to read or watch a movie, and relaxing seems hard and out of reach.

However, research has shown that just taking time each day, even for a few minutes, to relax, can have many benefits to our health, and can greatly improve our lives.

The Secret Colouring Book,

This is The Best Colouring Book For Adults, A True Art Therapy Colouring Book For Grownups.

50 New and Original Images.
Pocket Size

Relaxing art therapy colouring for people who love to relax

50 of the Best Images Carefully Created to Reduce Anxiety.

ISBN-13:
978-1517203559

ISBN-10:
1517203554

Copyright @ 2016 Clara E Brown
All Rights Reserved

The connection between art and hypnotic trance state is well known, and today we understand that colouring allows us to leave our worries behind and enter into our own hypnotic state of trance.

We understand the meaning of Art Therapy and know it is used to alleviate both physical and mental health problems.

When we colour our minds are free to enter into a hypnotic trance, we go into a relaxed state as we concentrate on our colouring. In effect we are tapping into our inner selves and accessing that side of us that is creative, calmer, stress free.

These images cannot be found elsewhere, each one is unique and as you choose your colours and let your mind focus in on your colouring, you will find yourself taking a break from your daily worries, you will find yourself relaxing and you have permission to let yourself relax and be happier in your life.

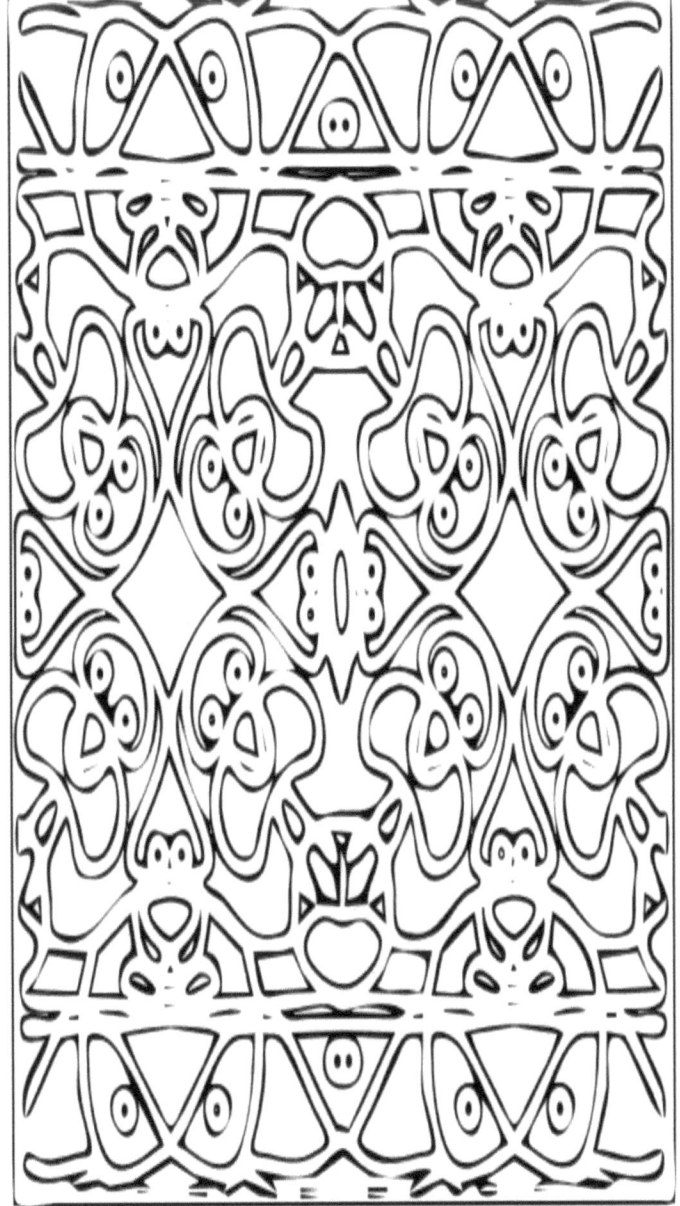

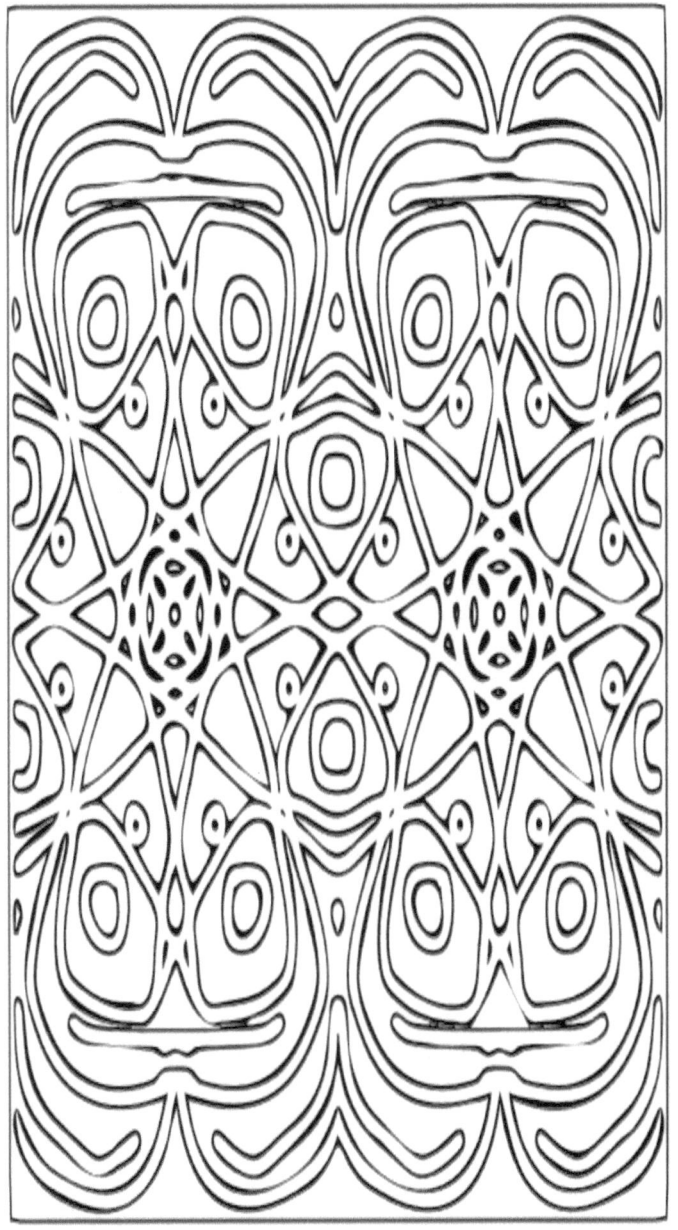

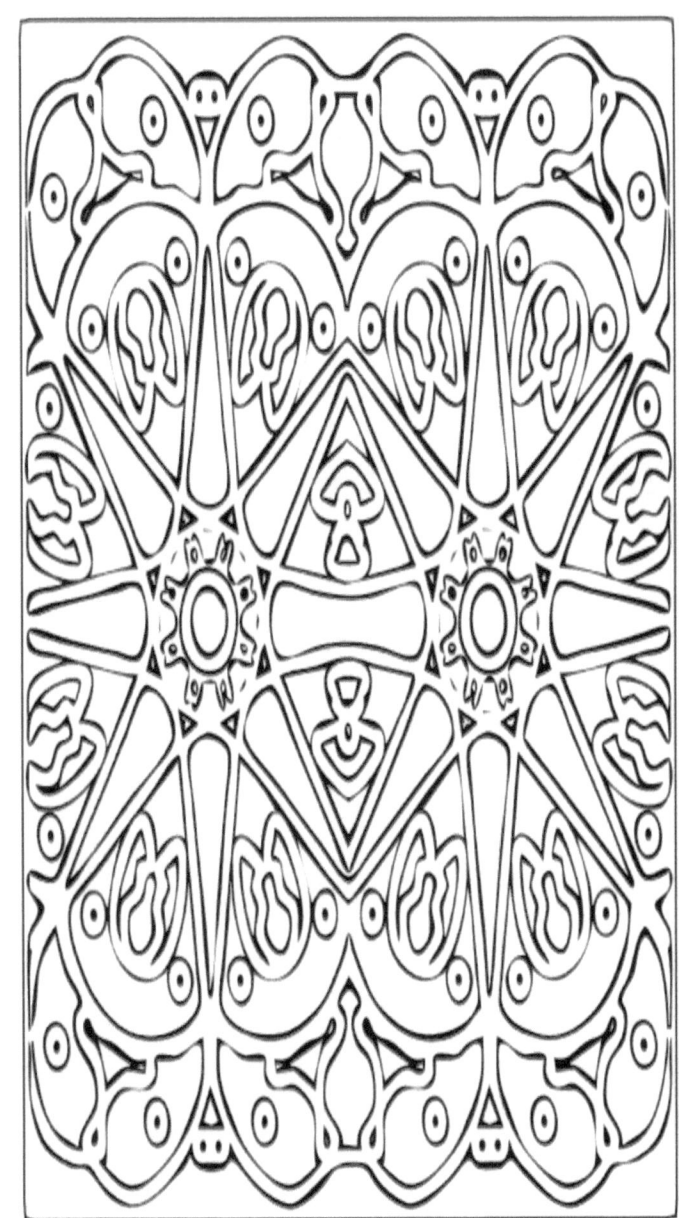

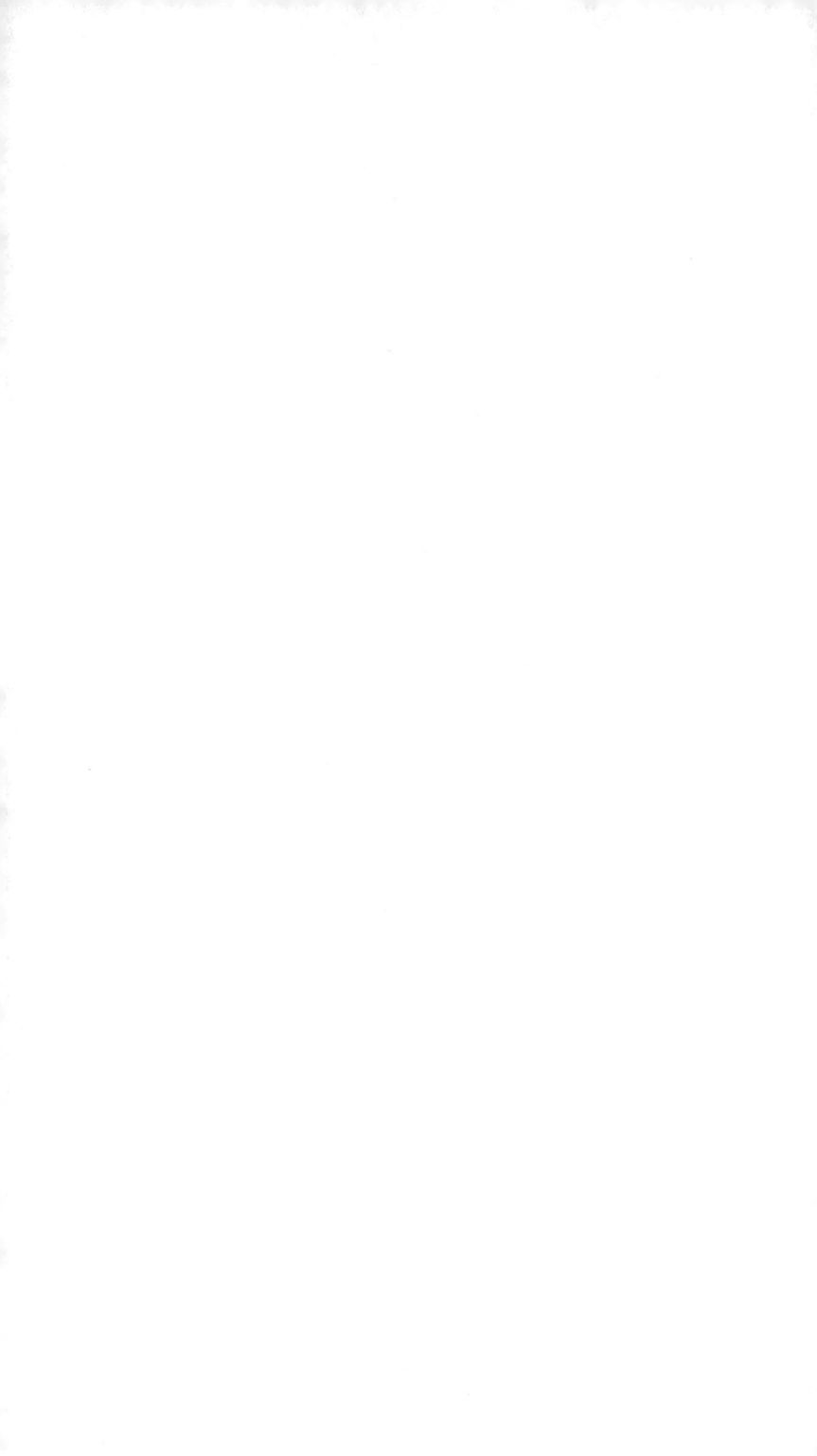

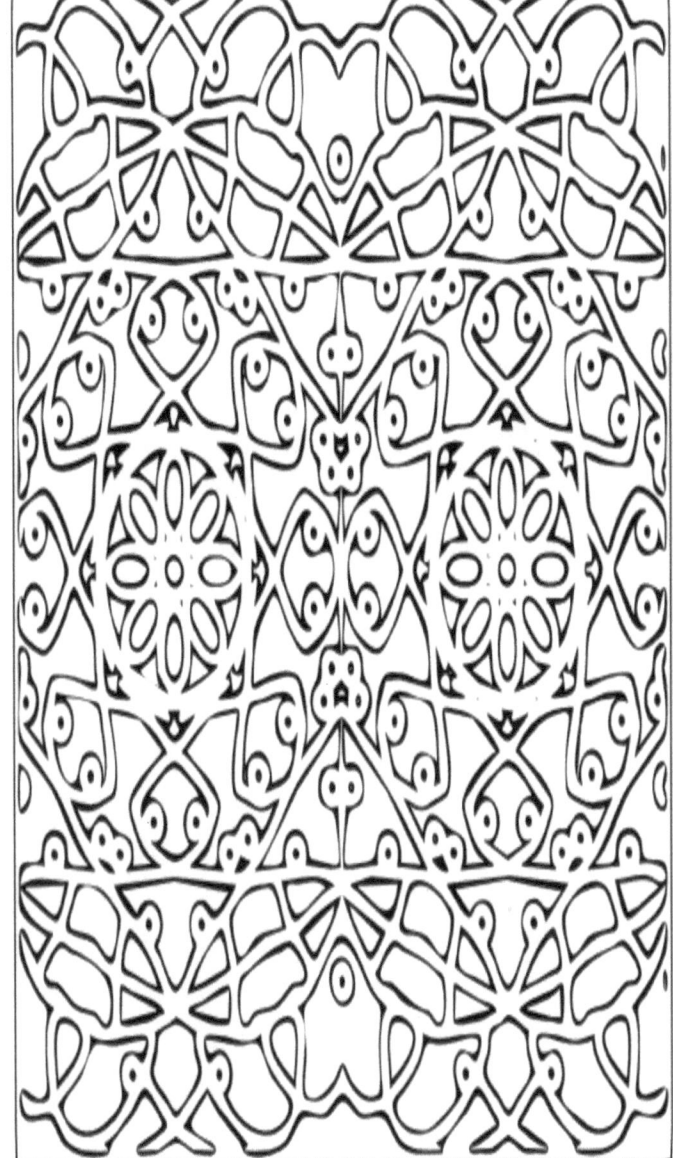

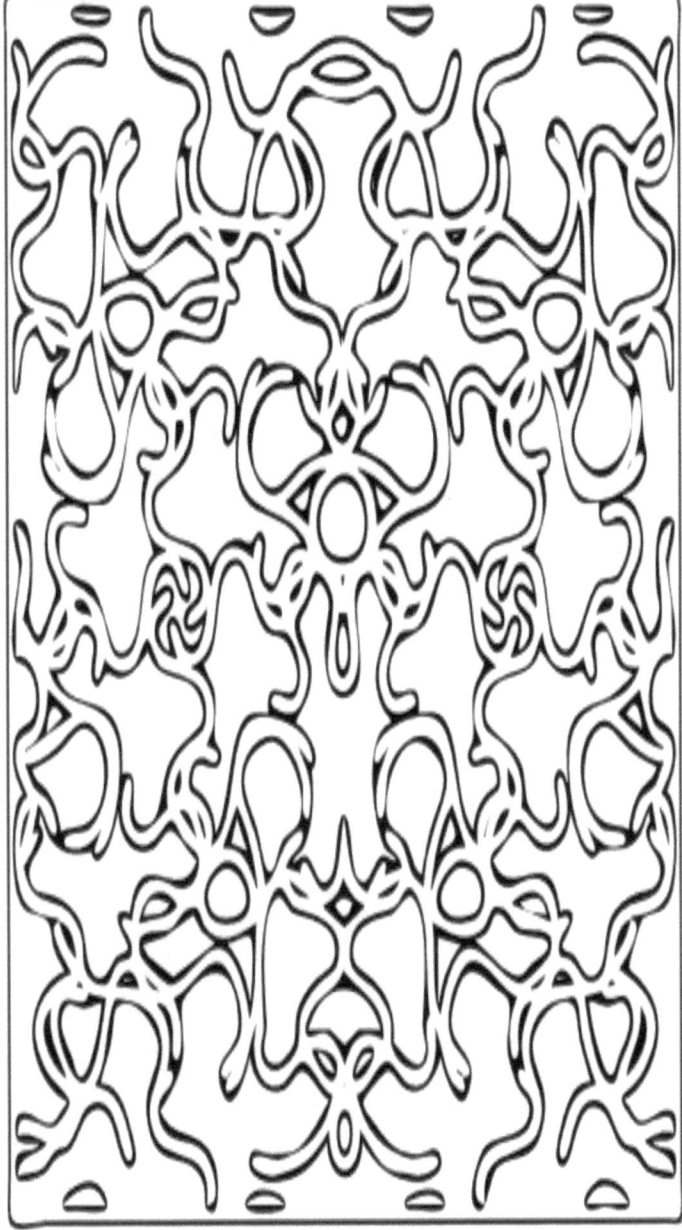

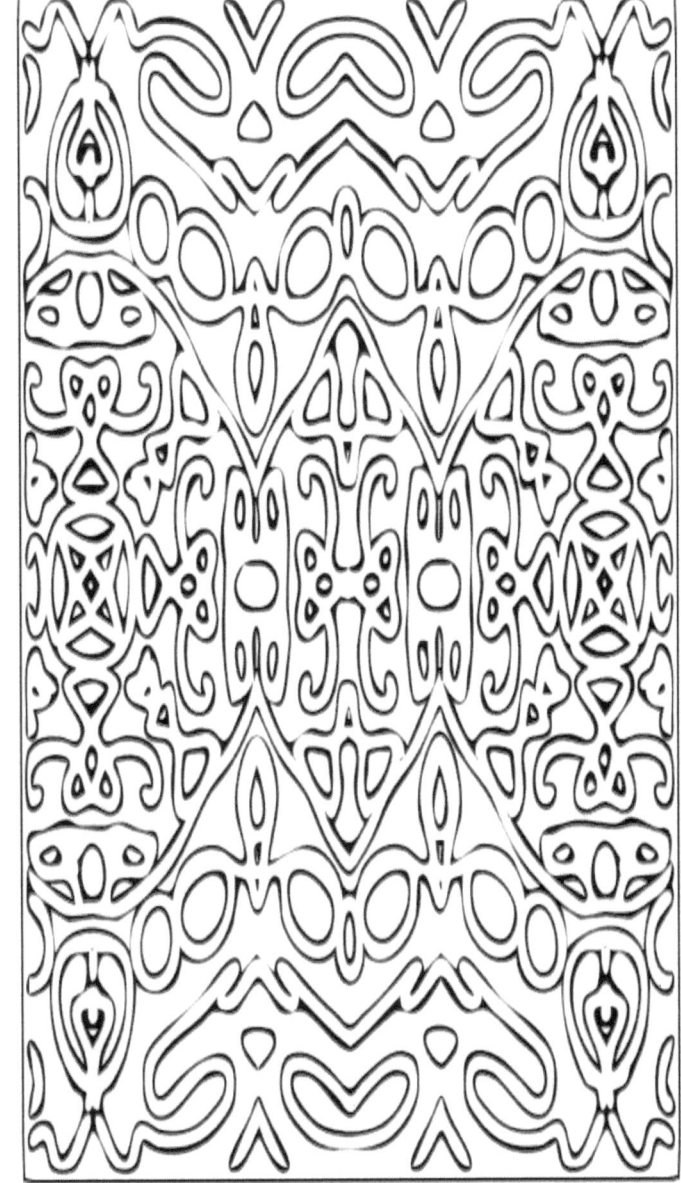

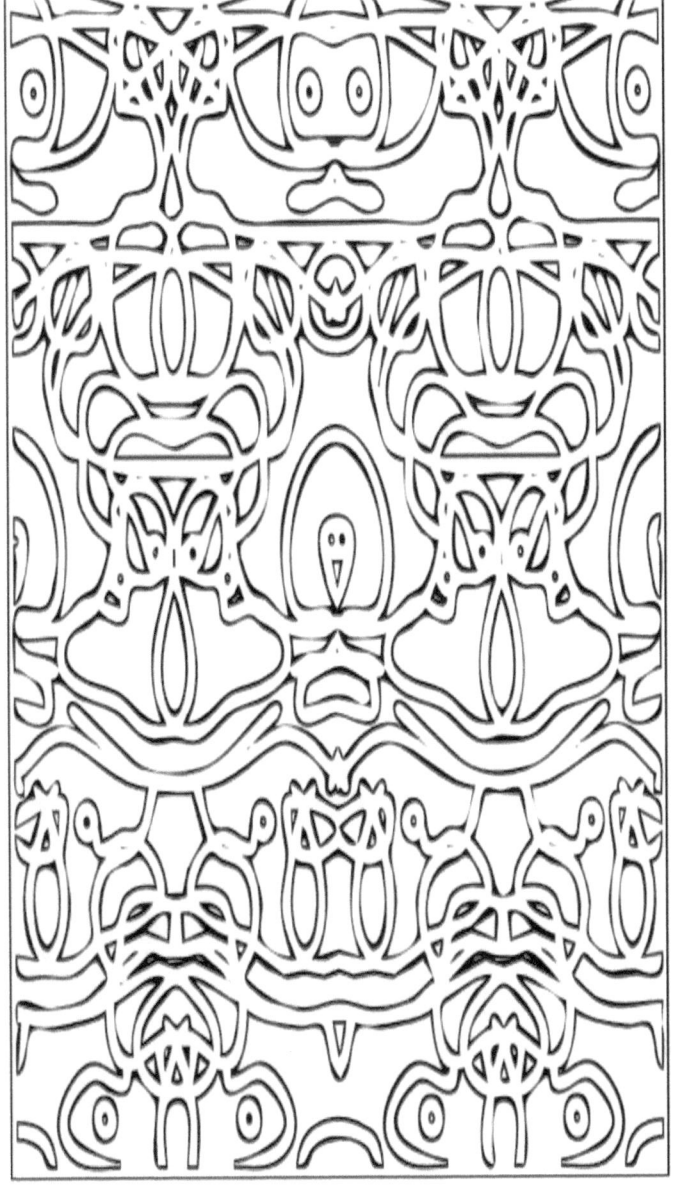

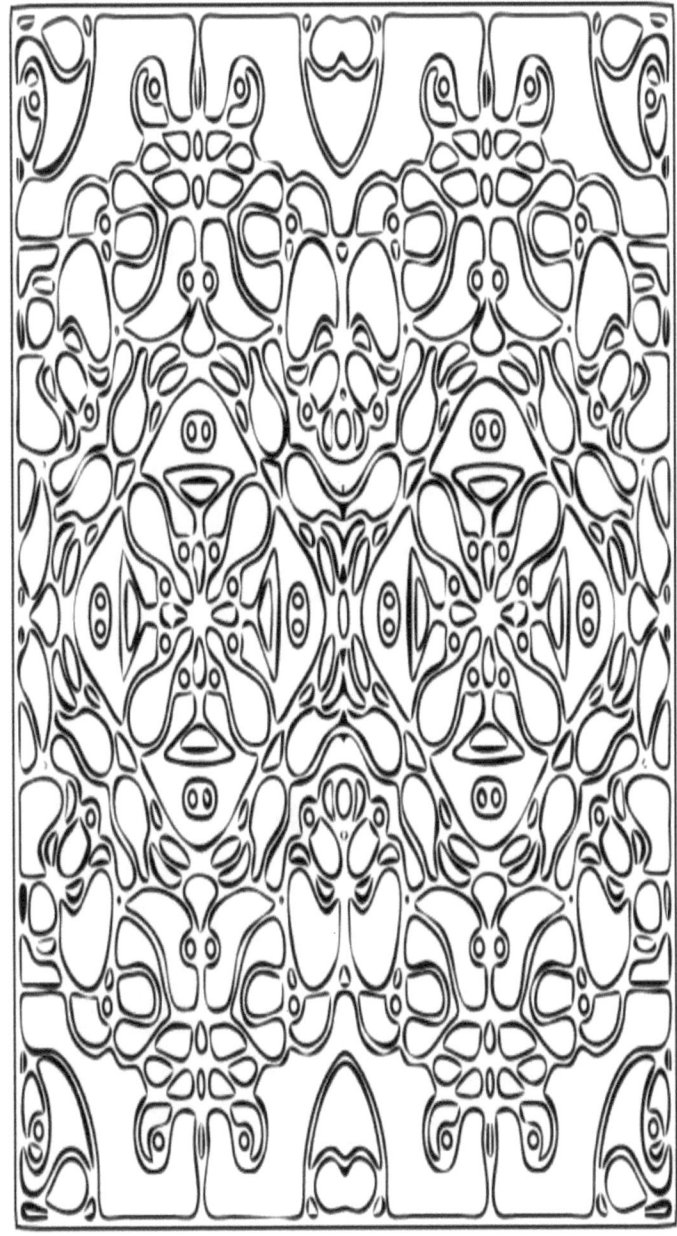

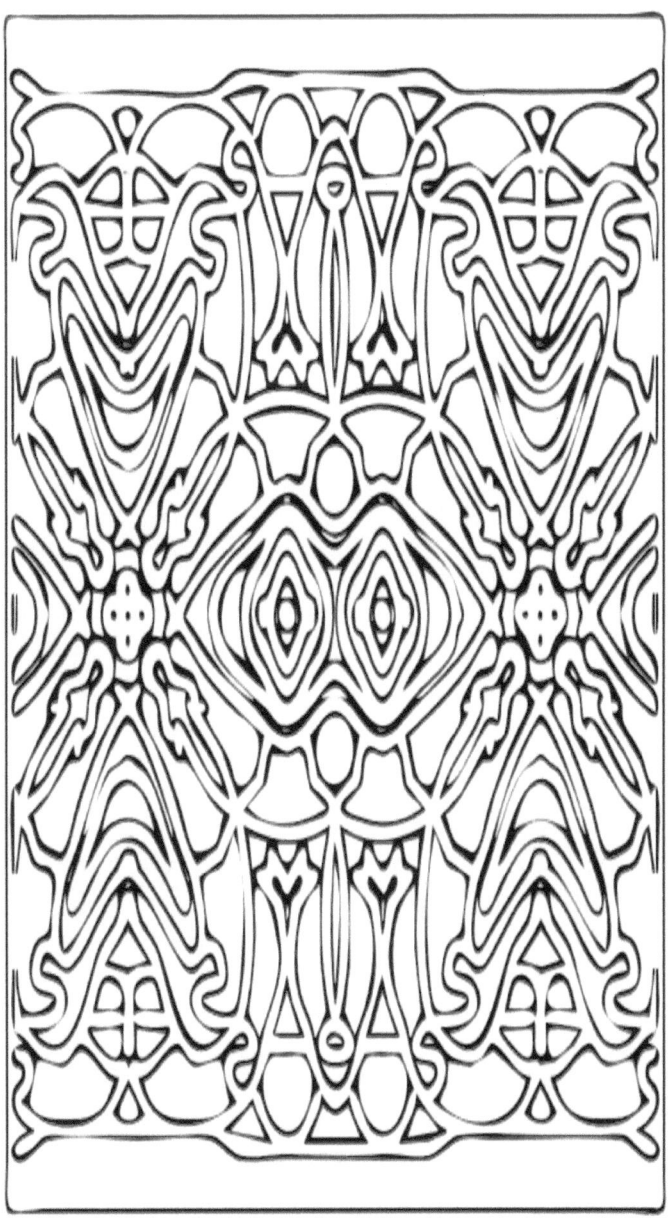

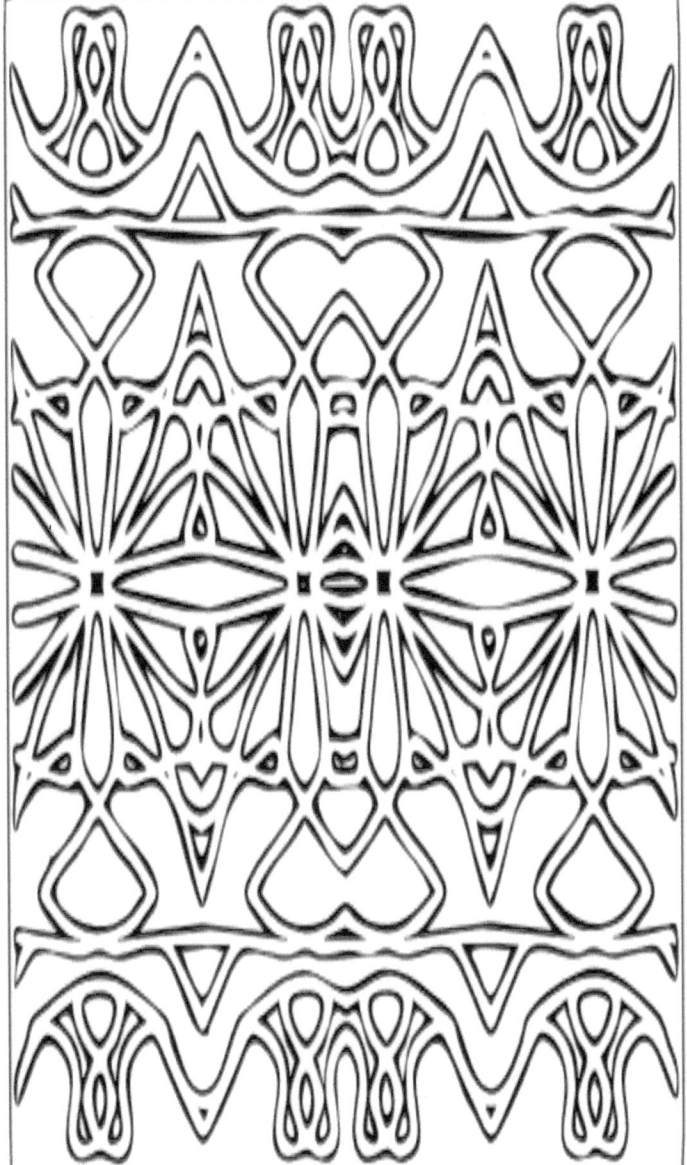

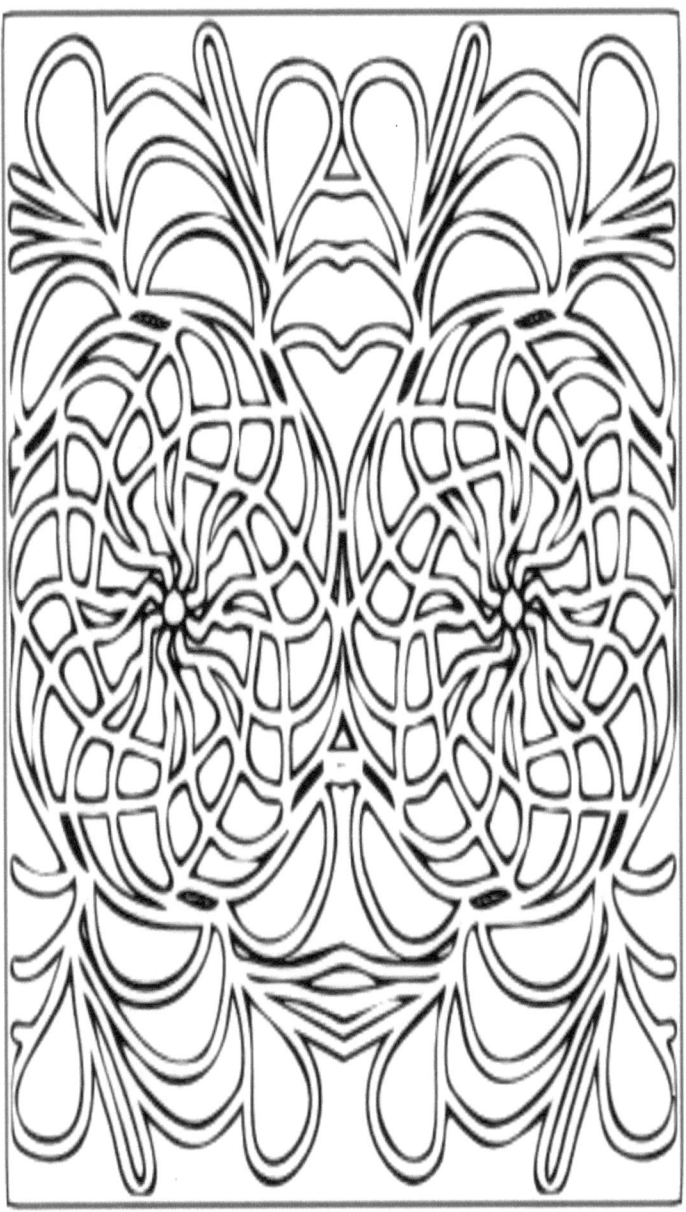

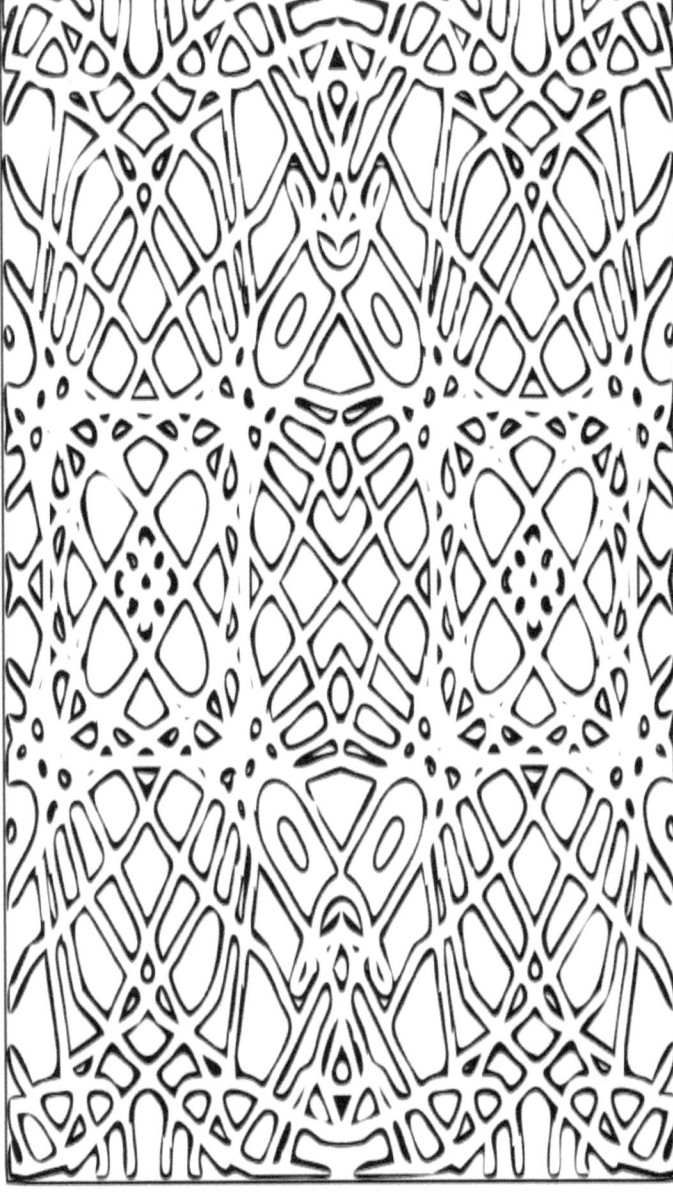

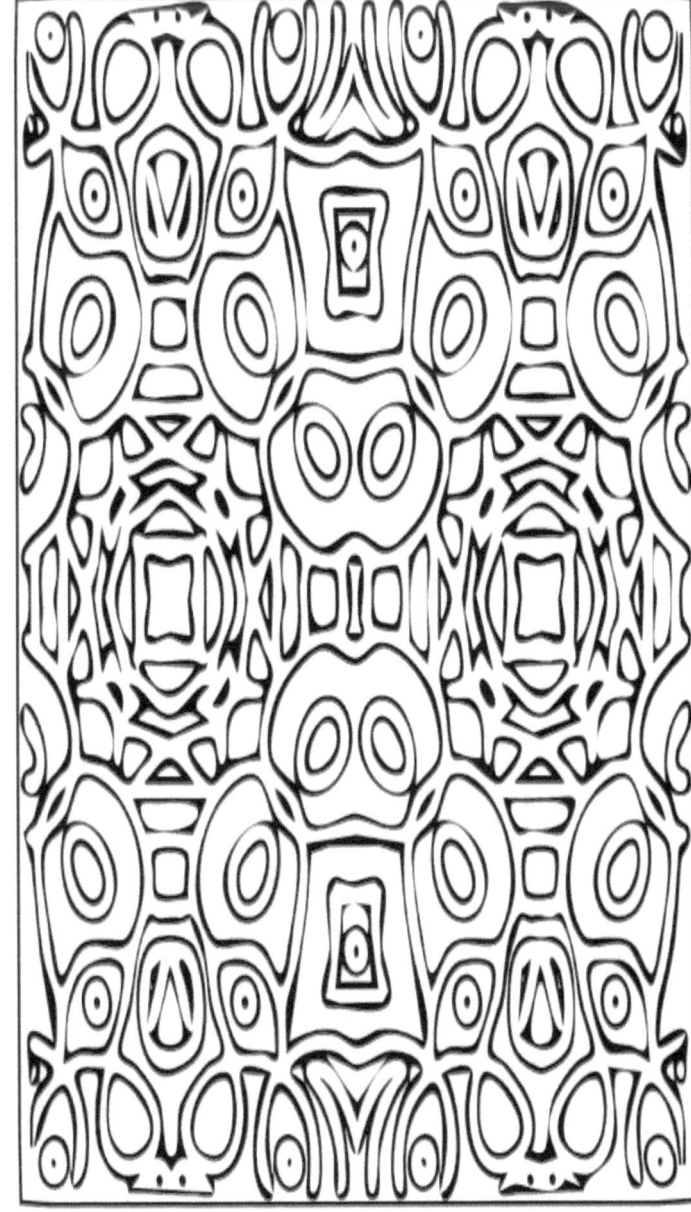

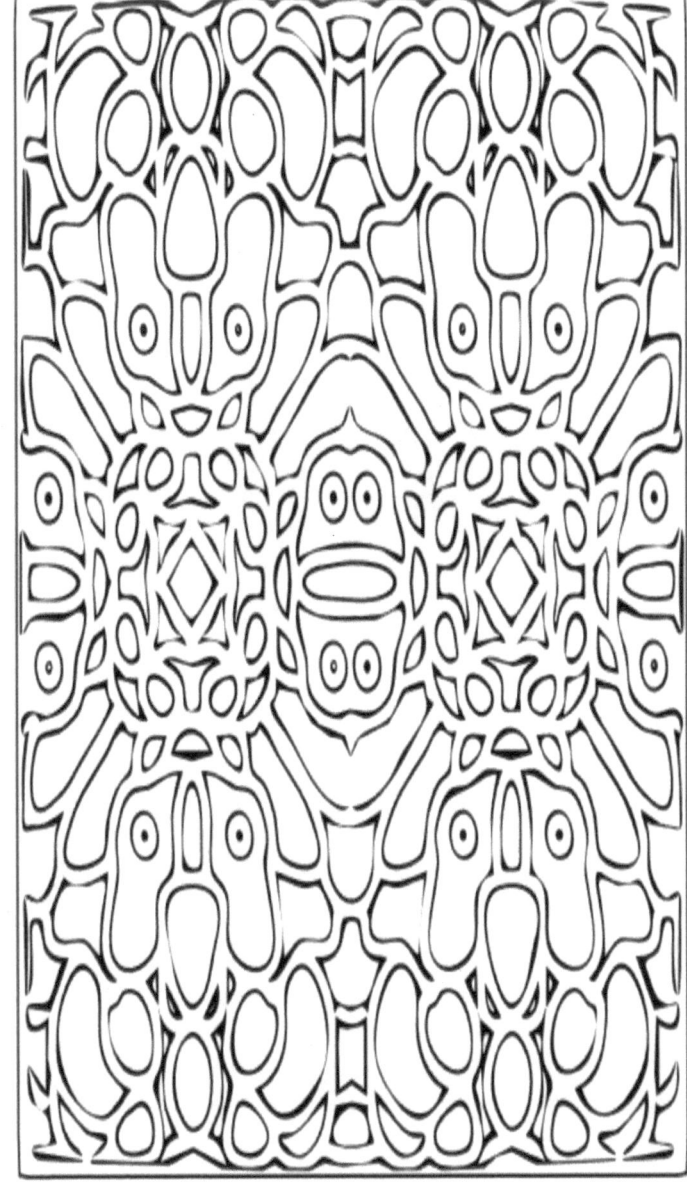

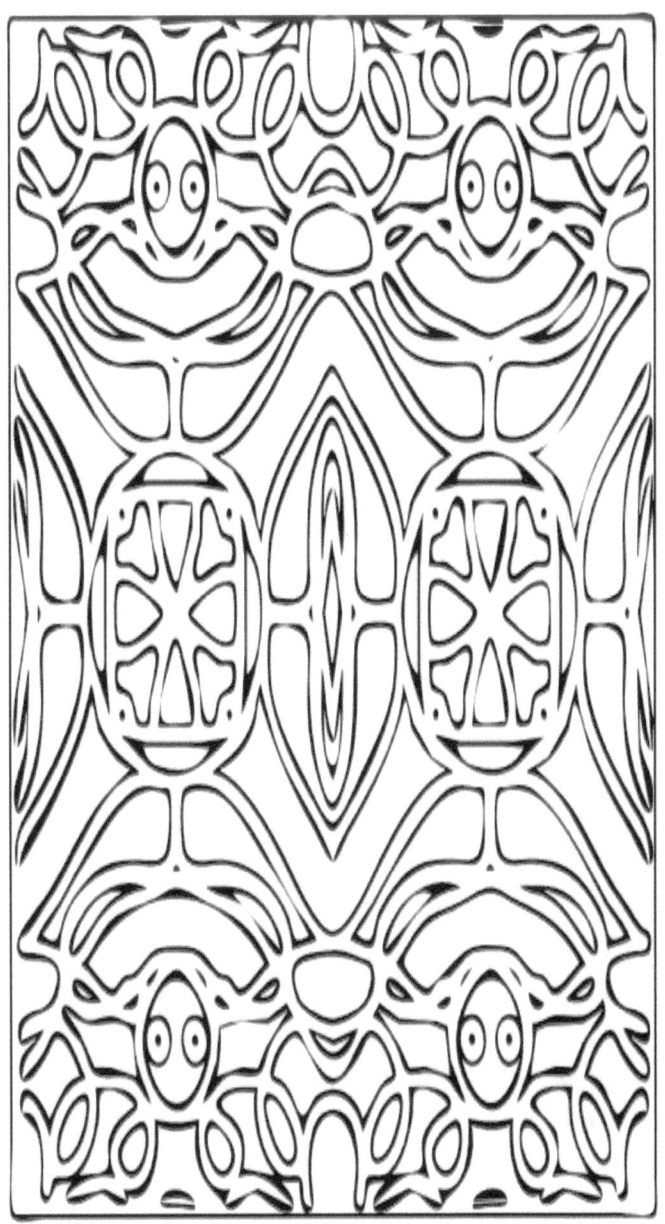

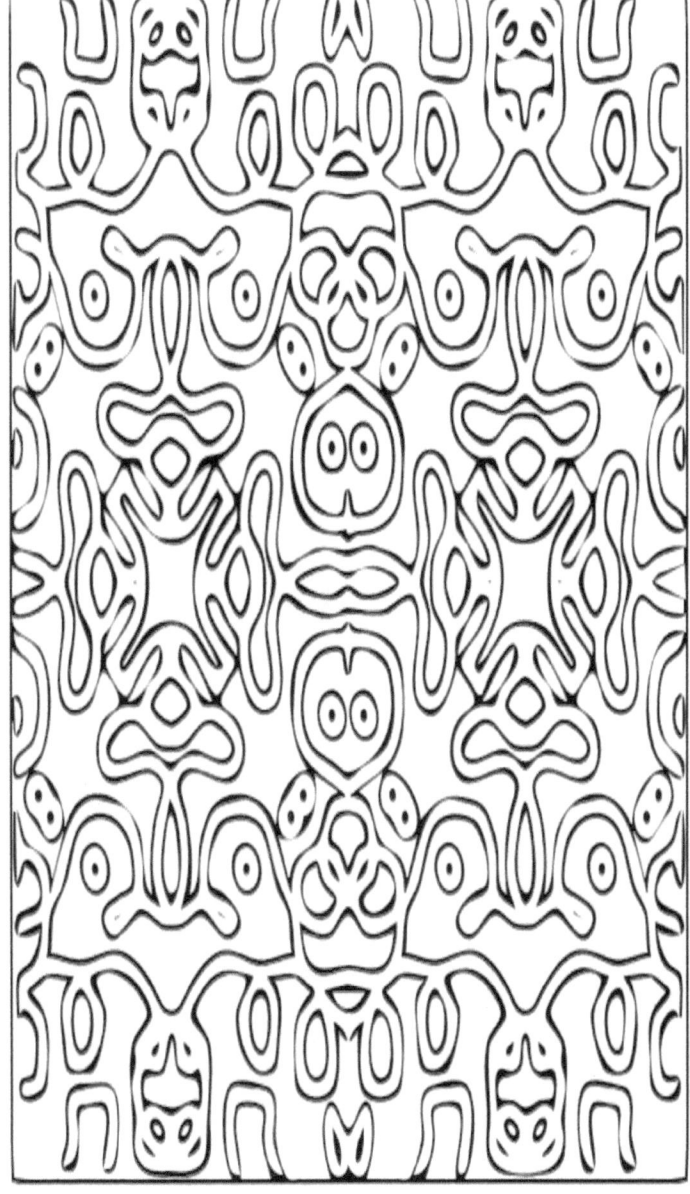

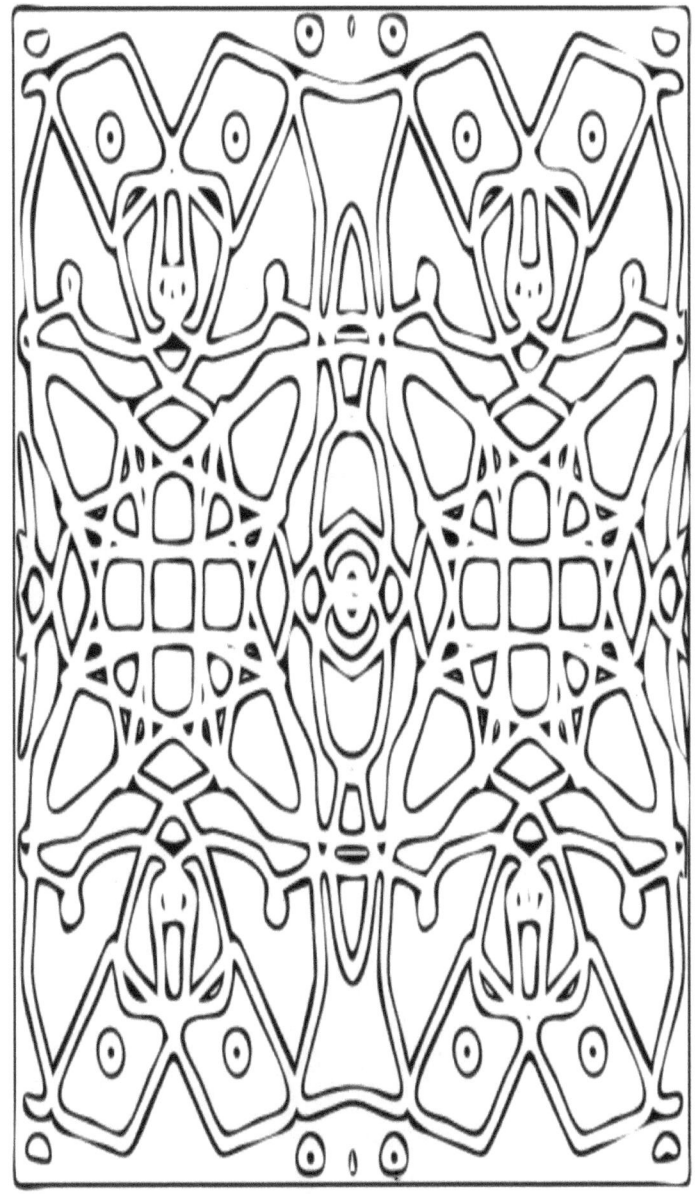

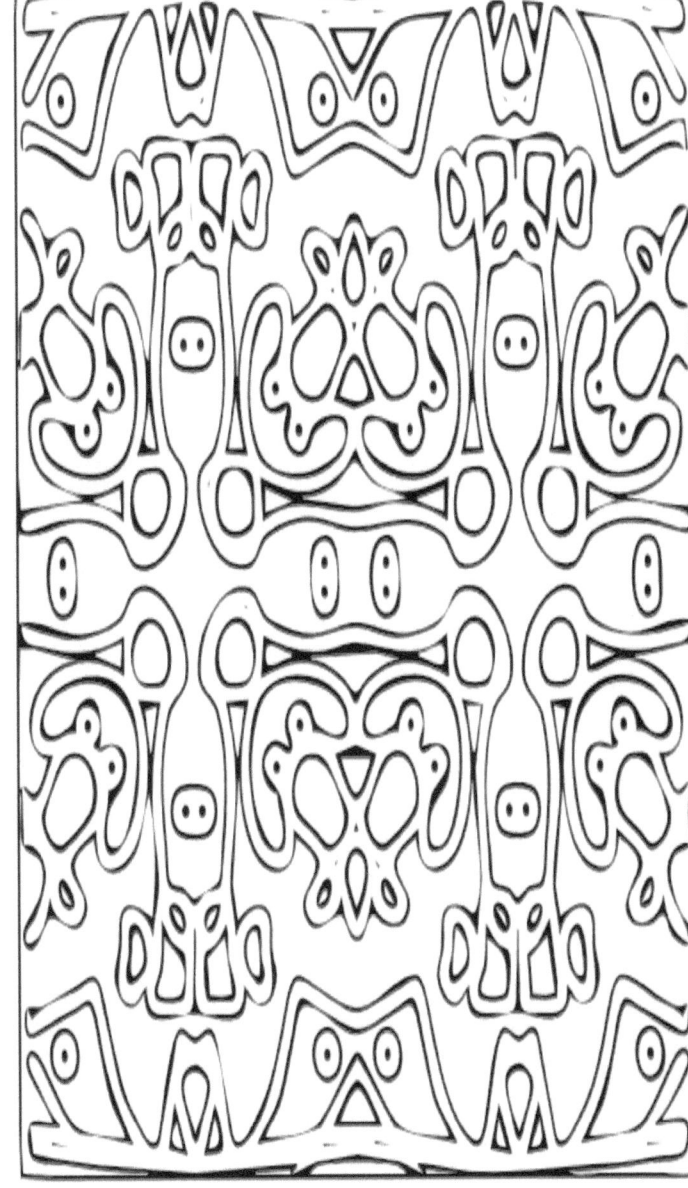

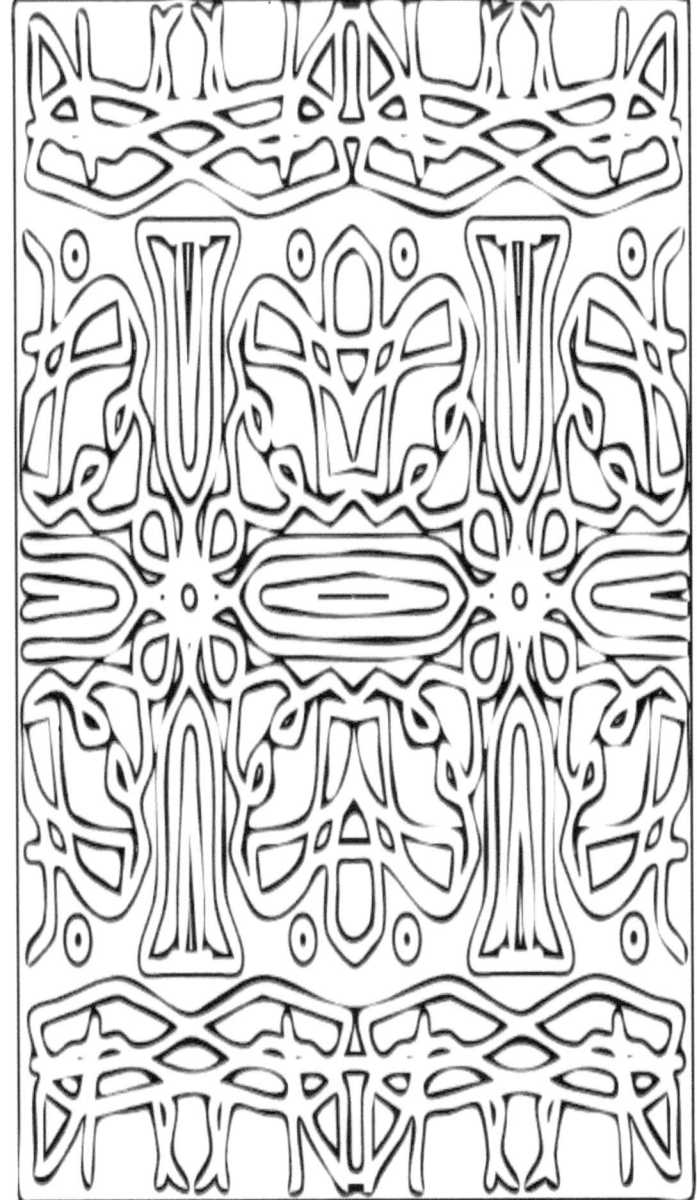

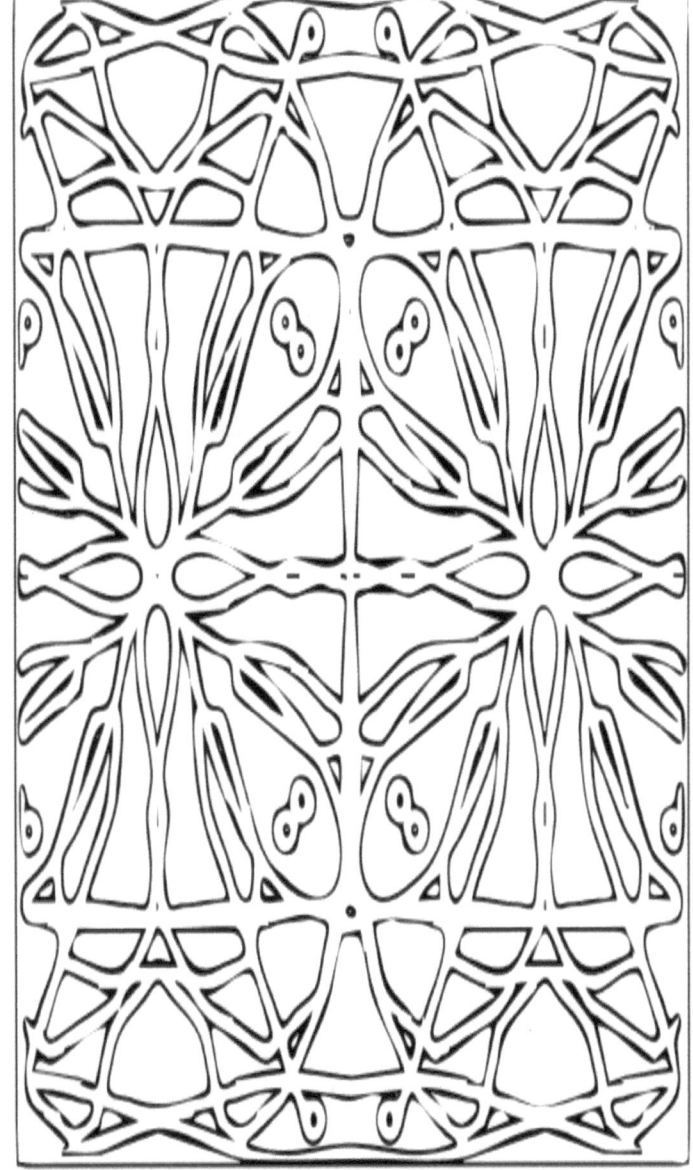

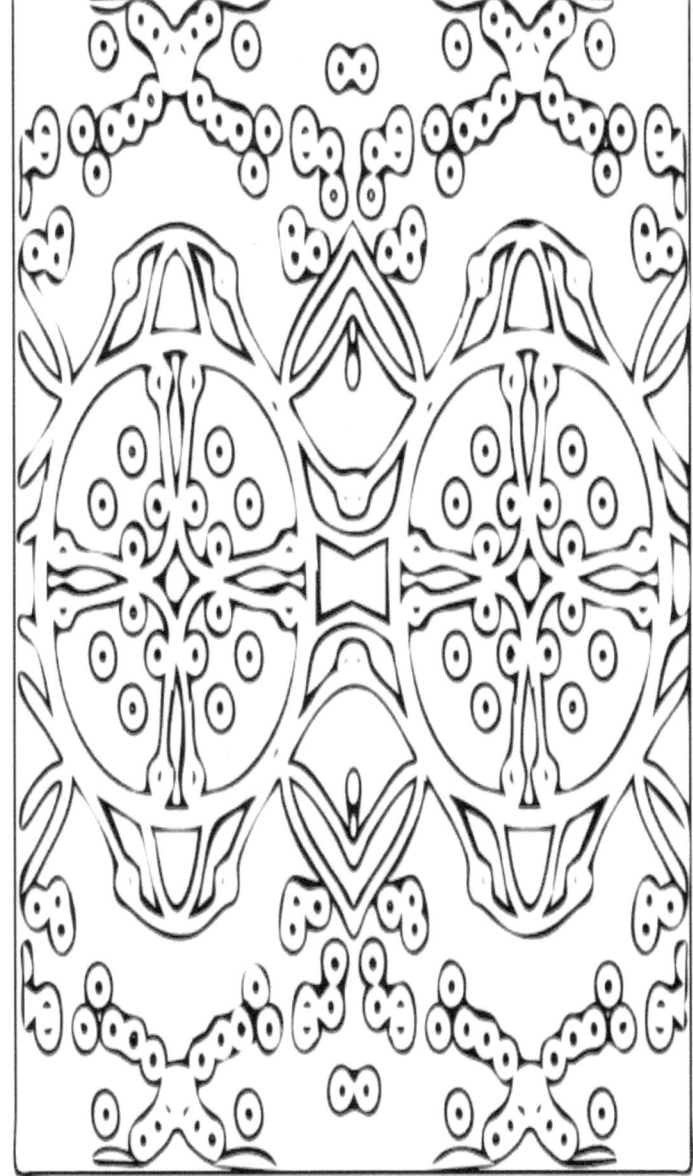

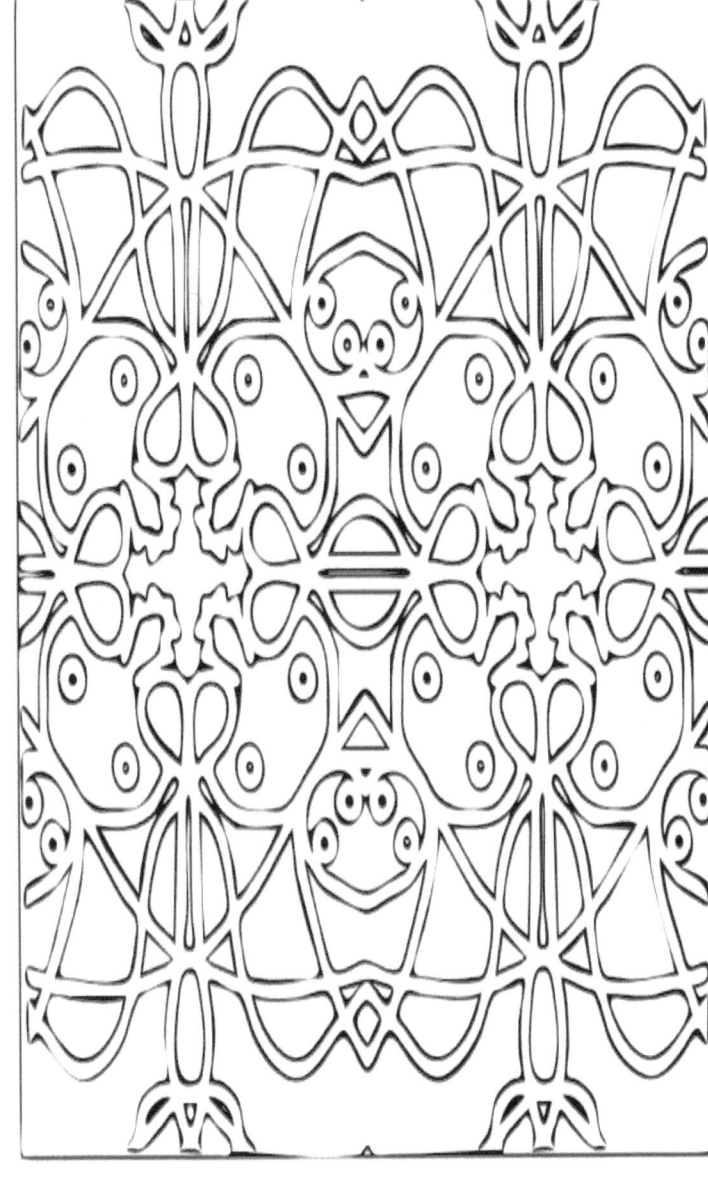

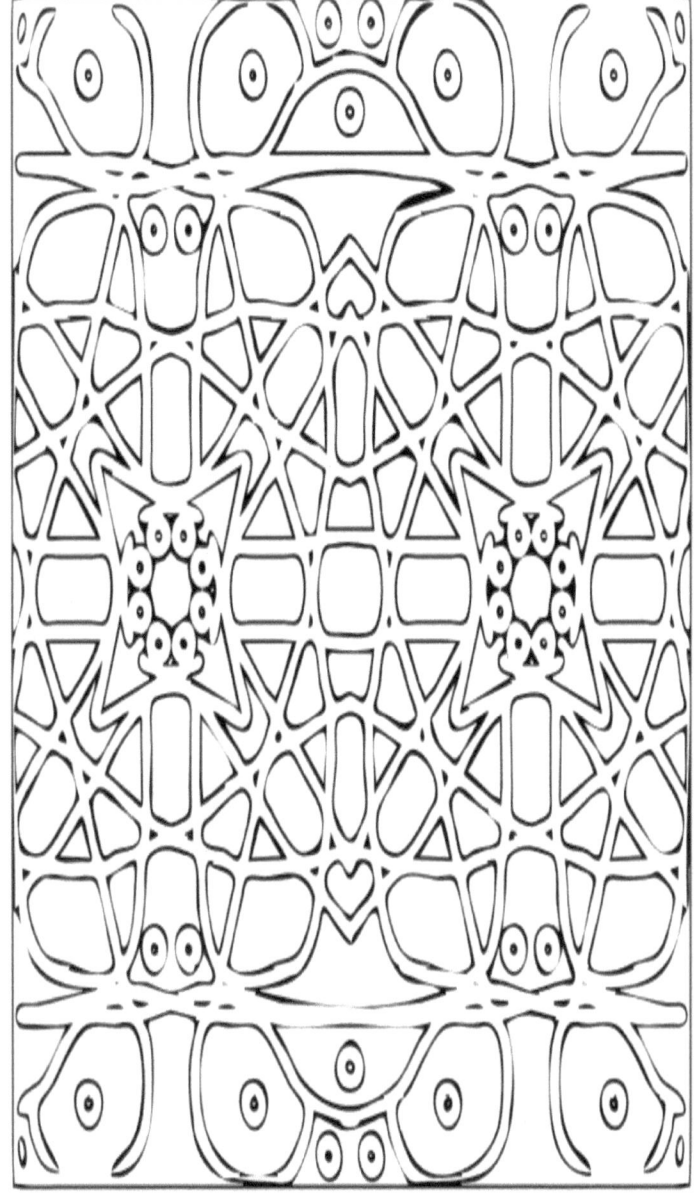

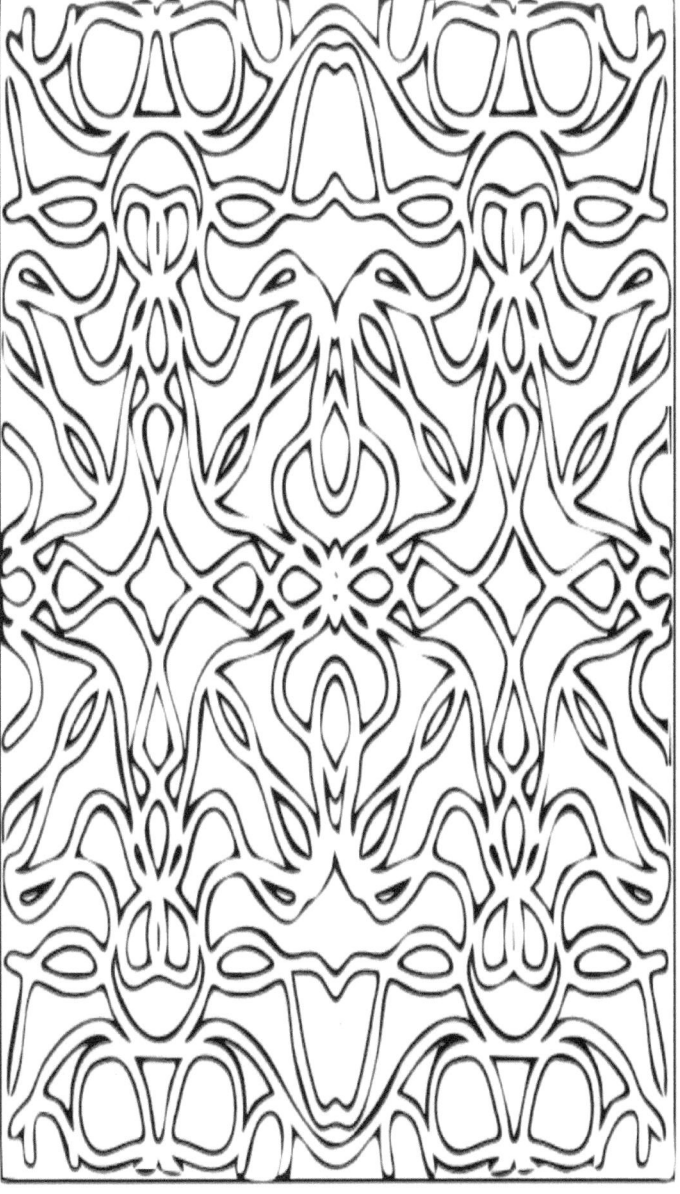

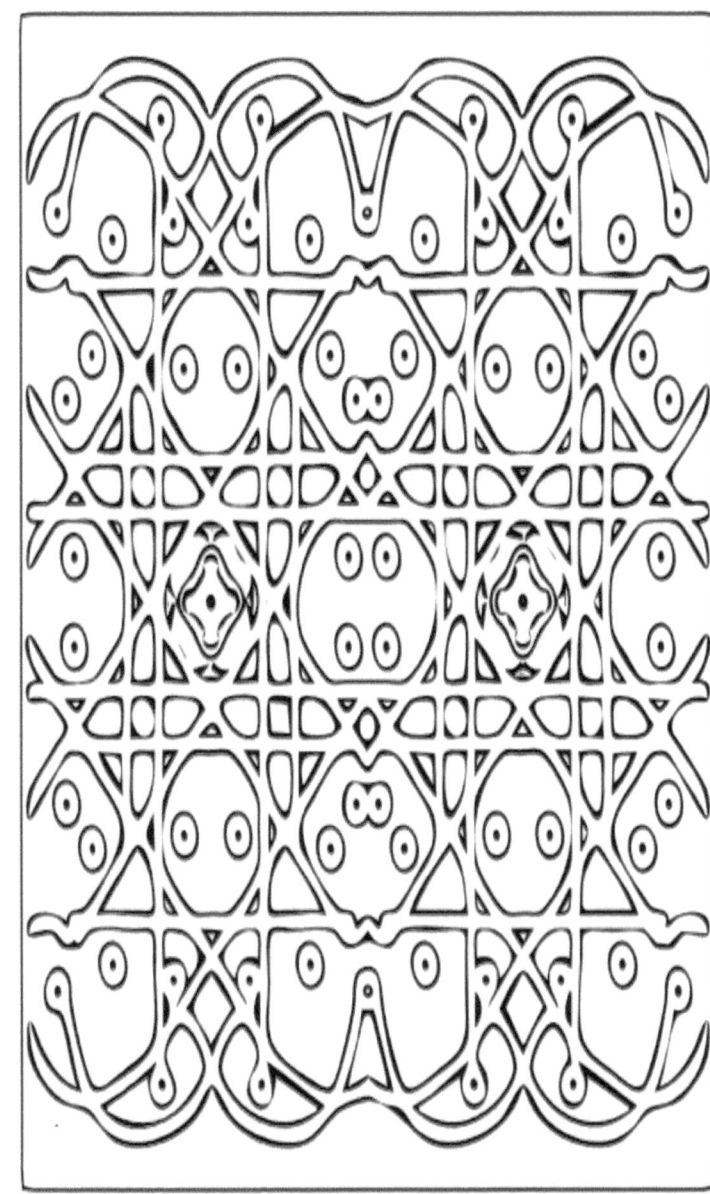

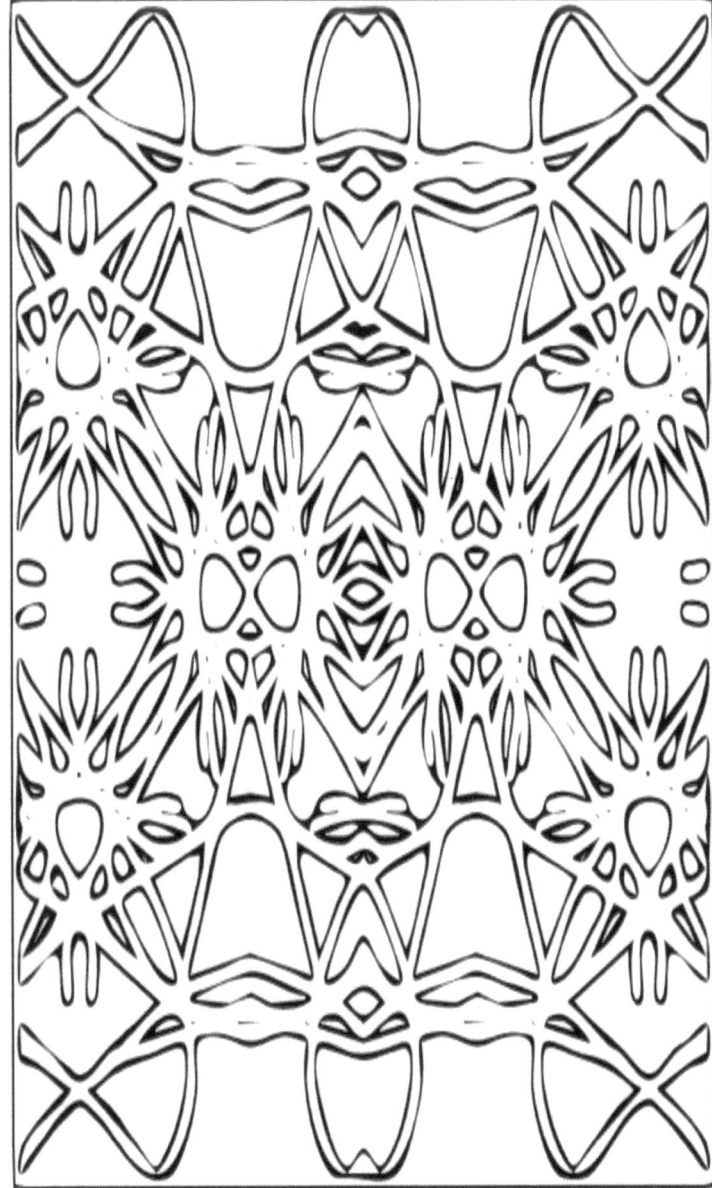

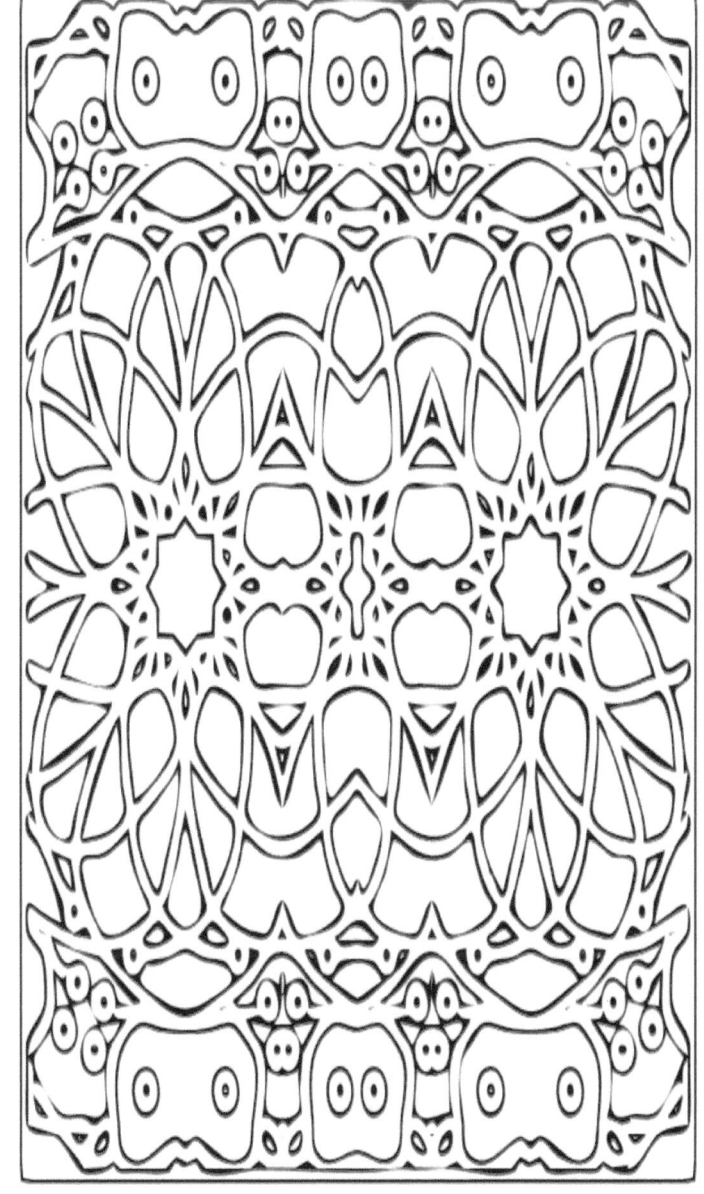

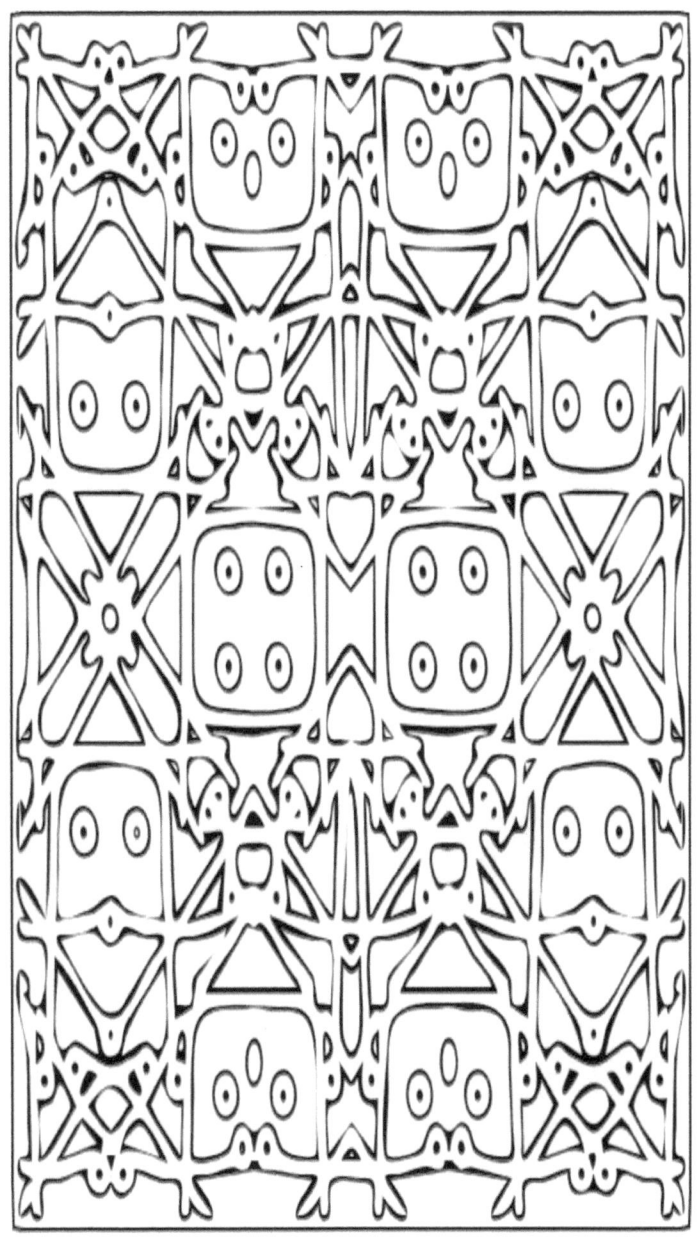

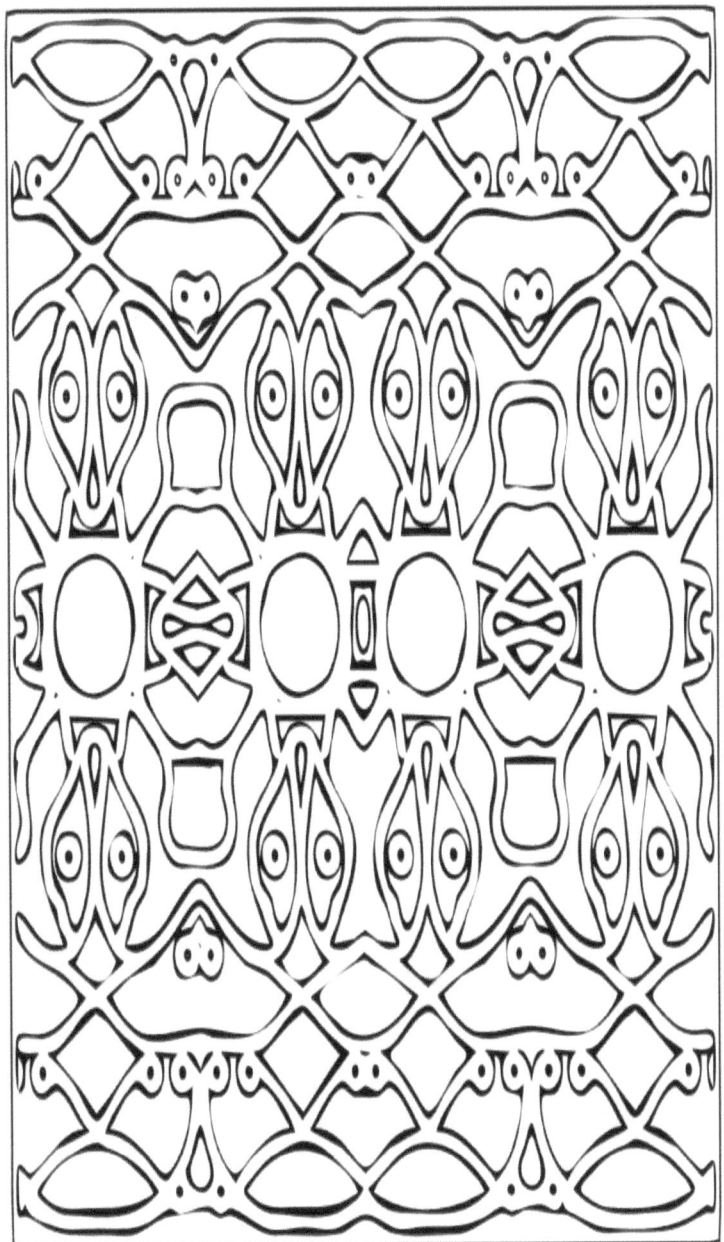

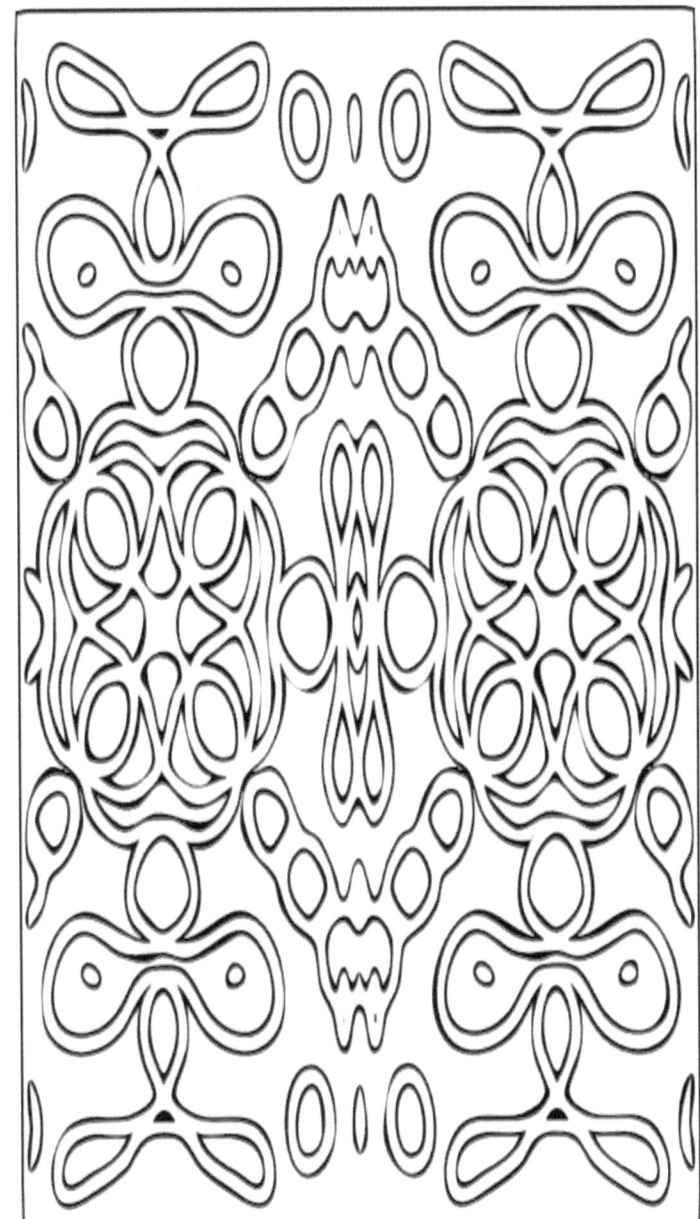

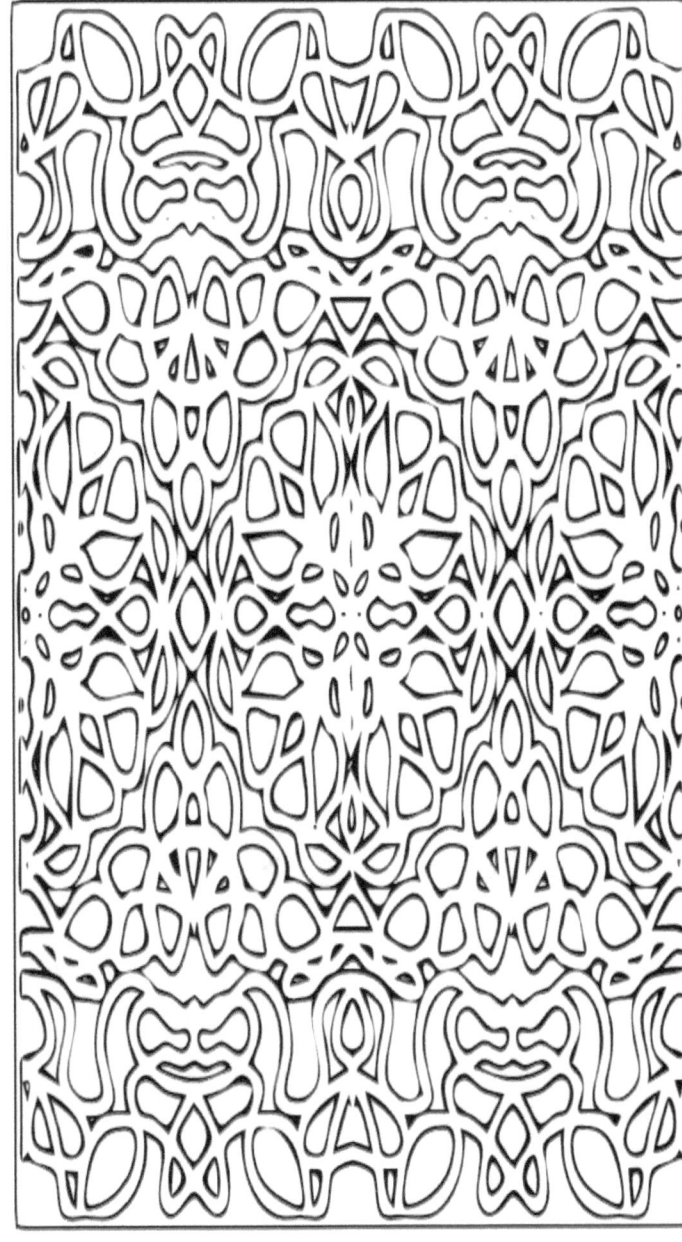

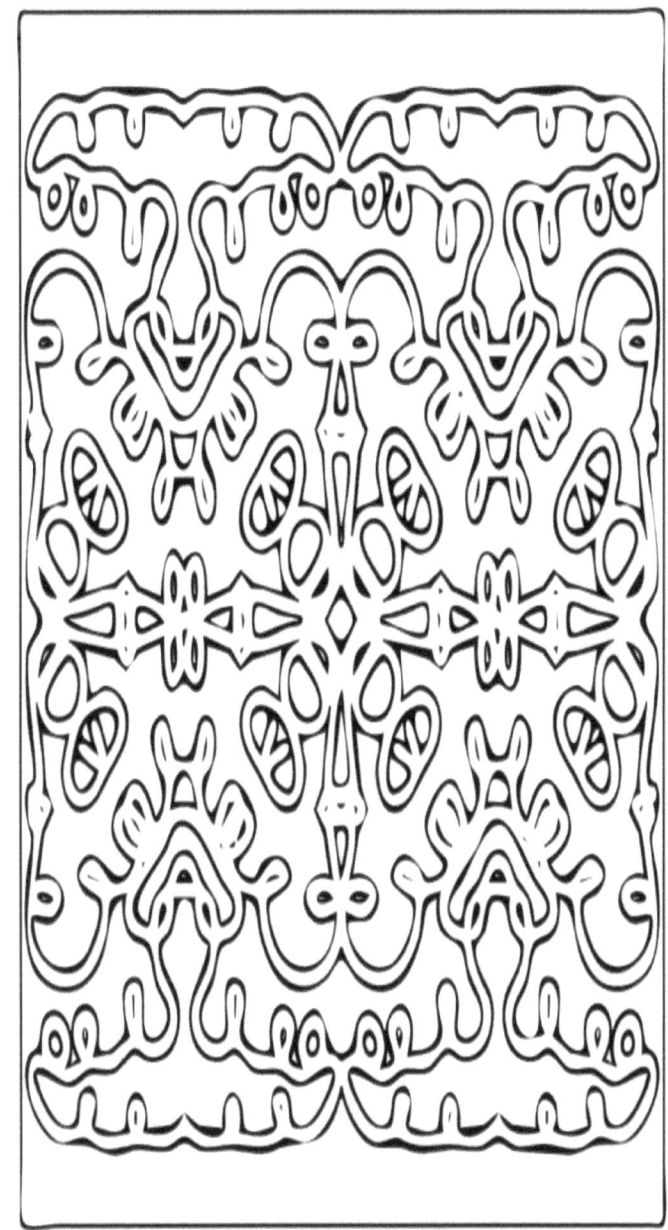

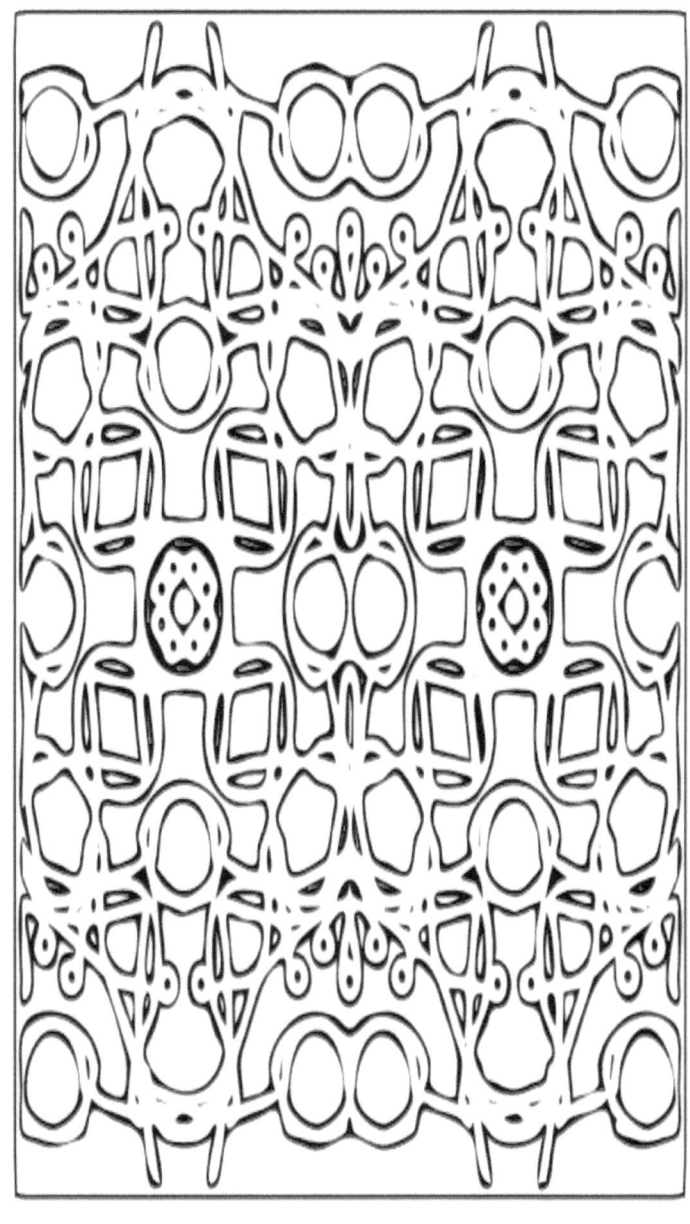

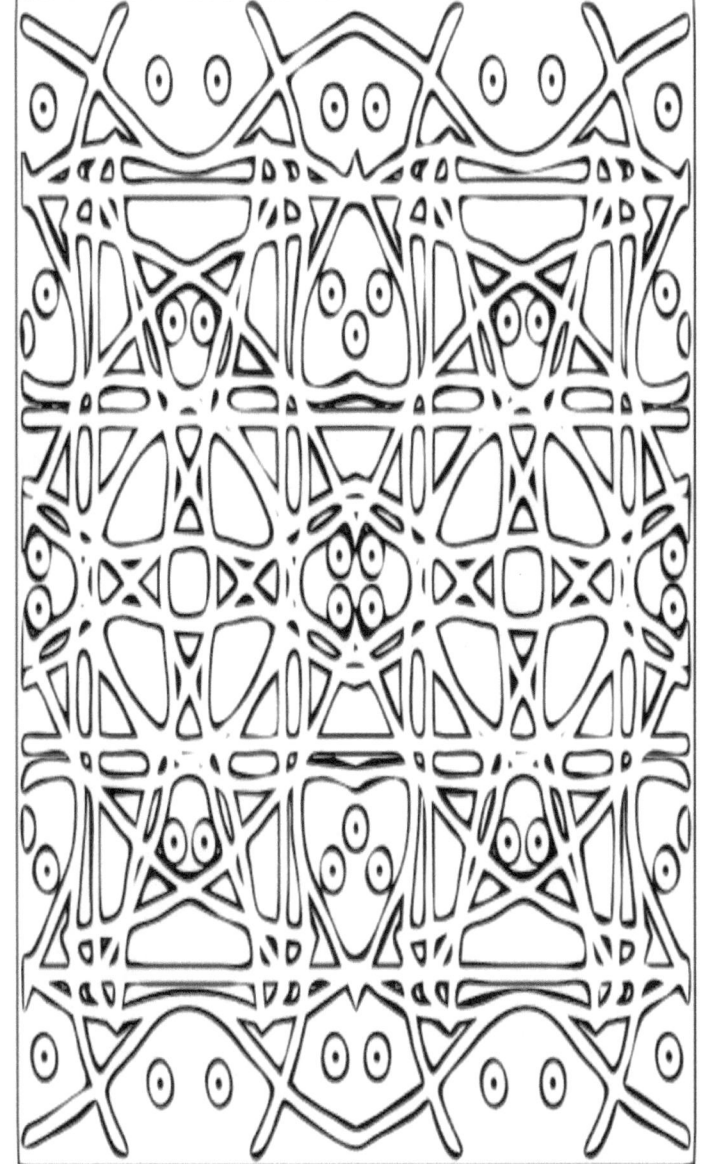

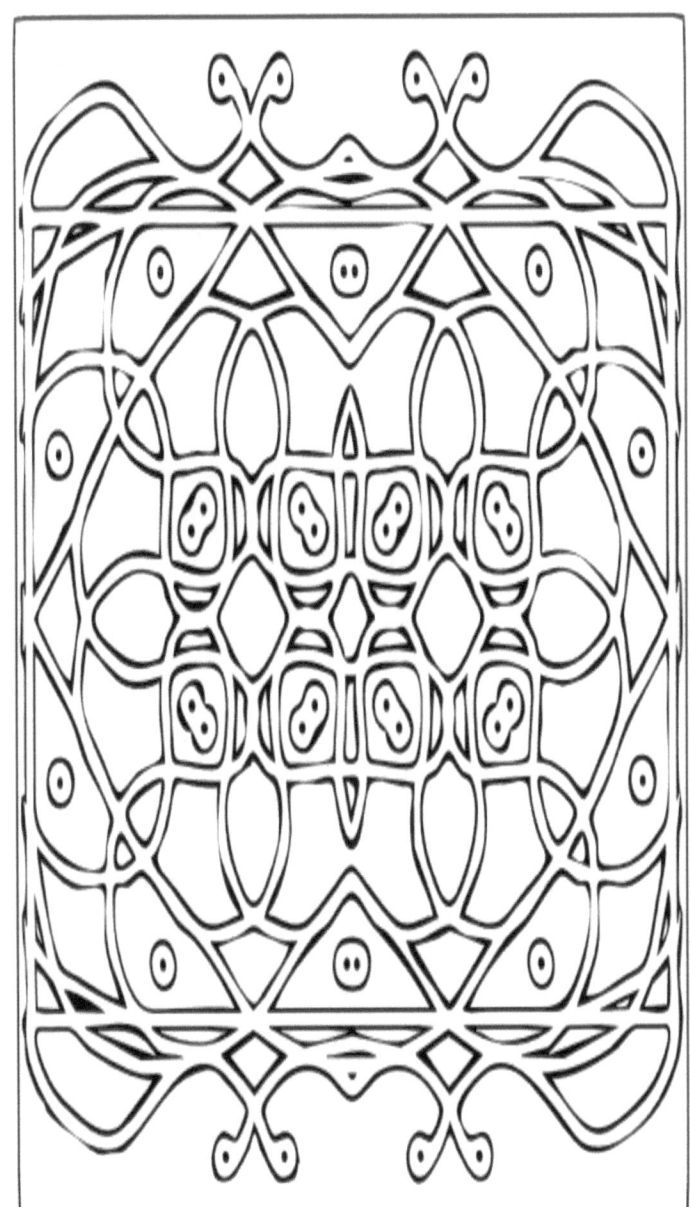

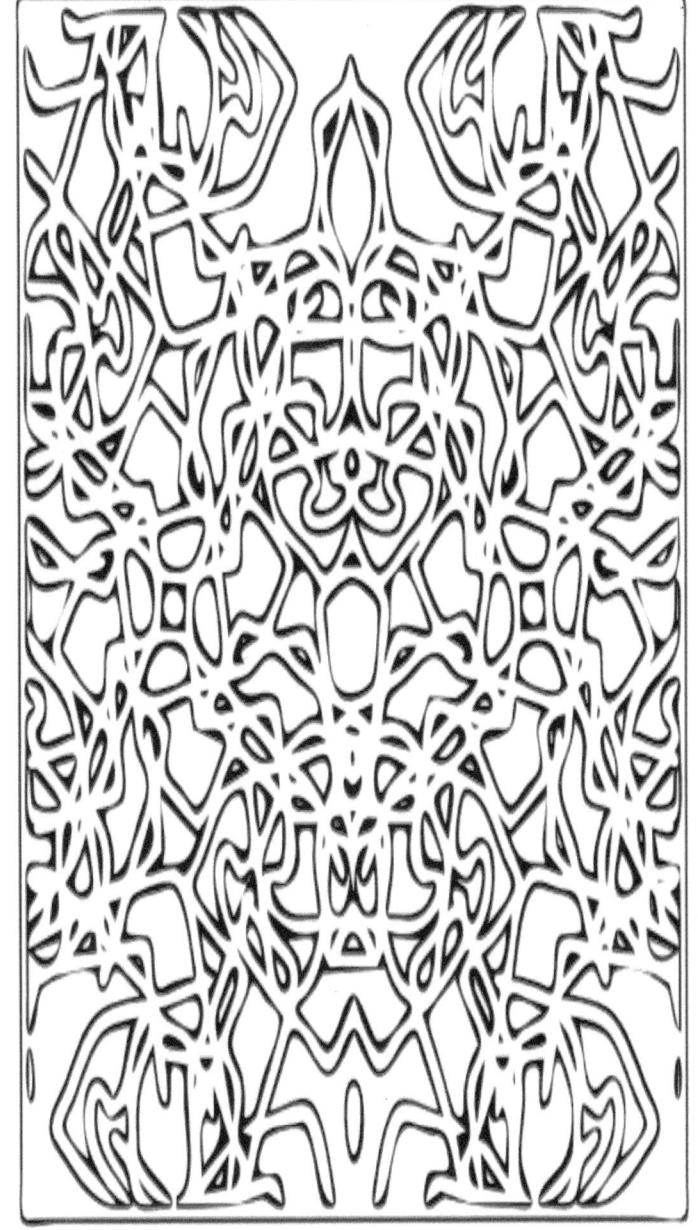

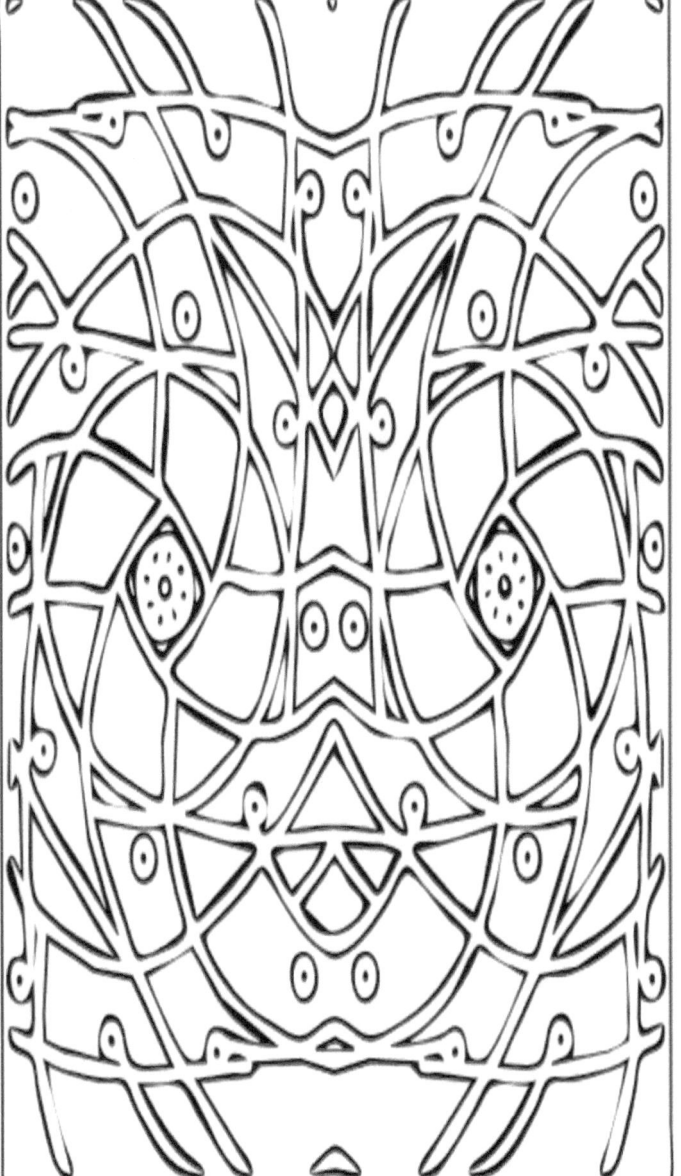

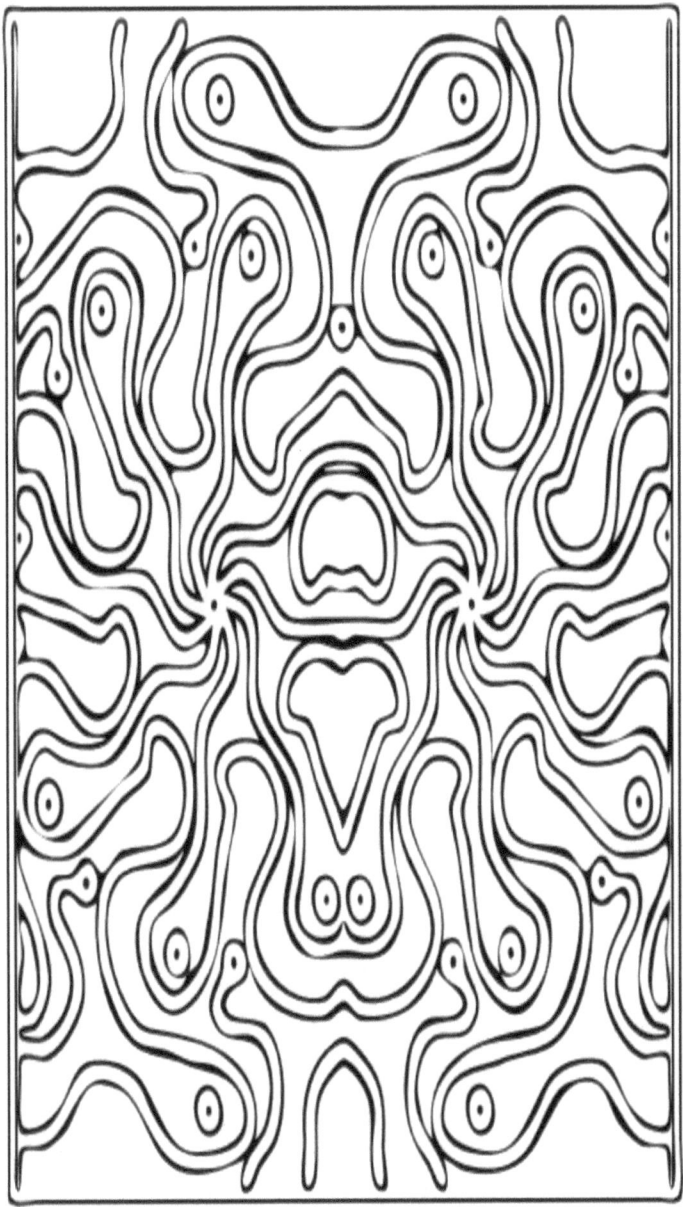

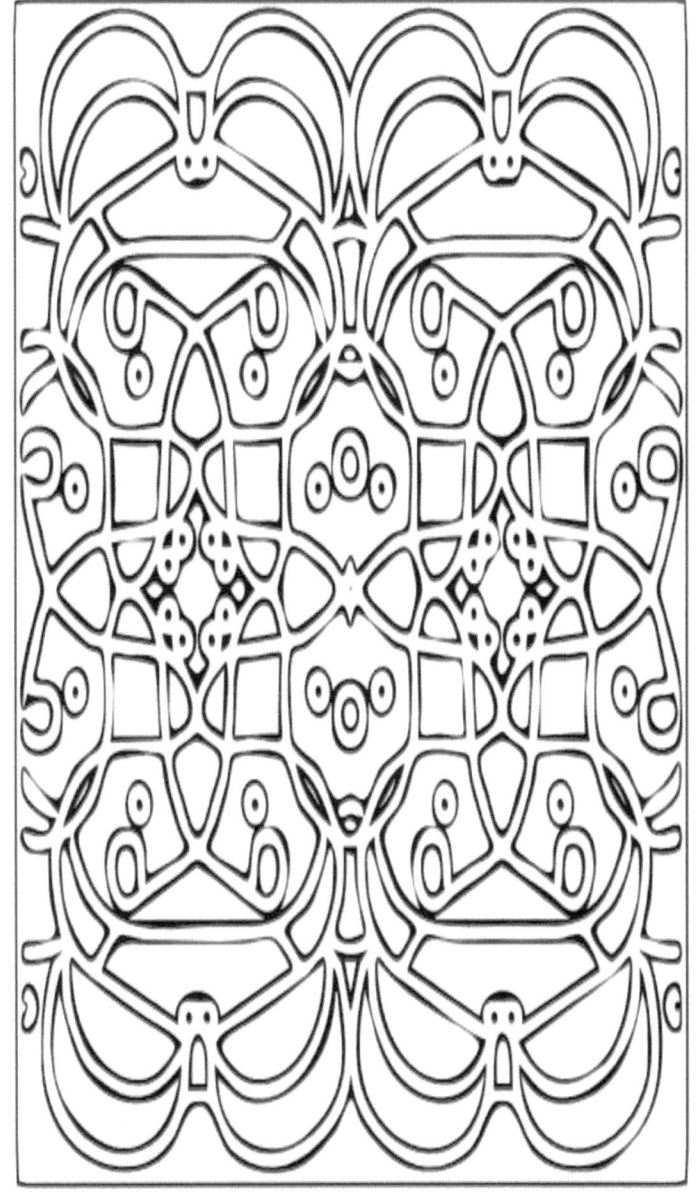

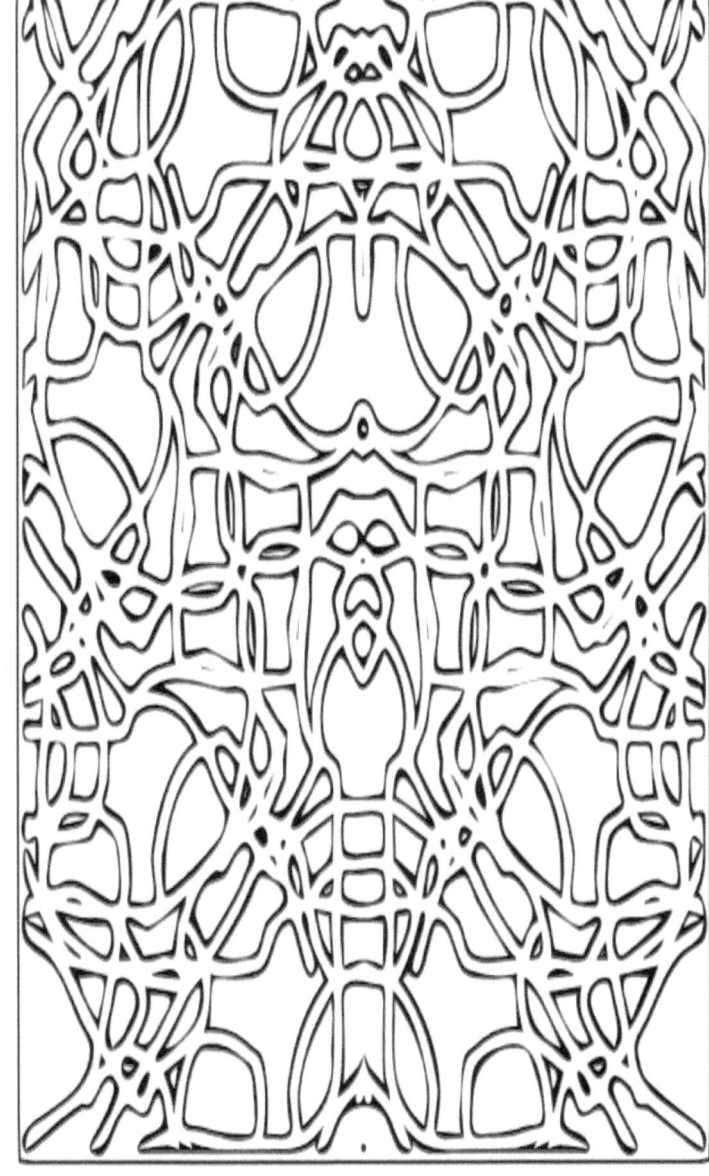

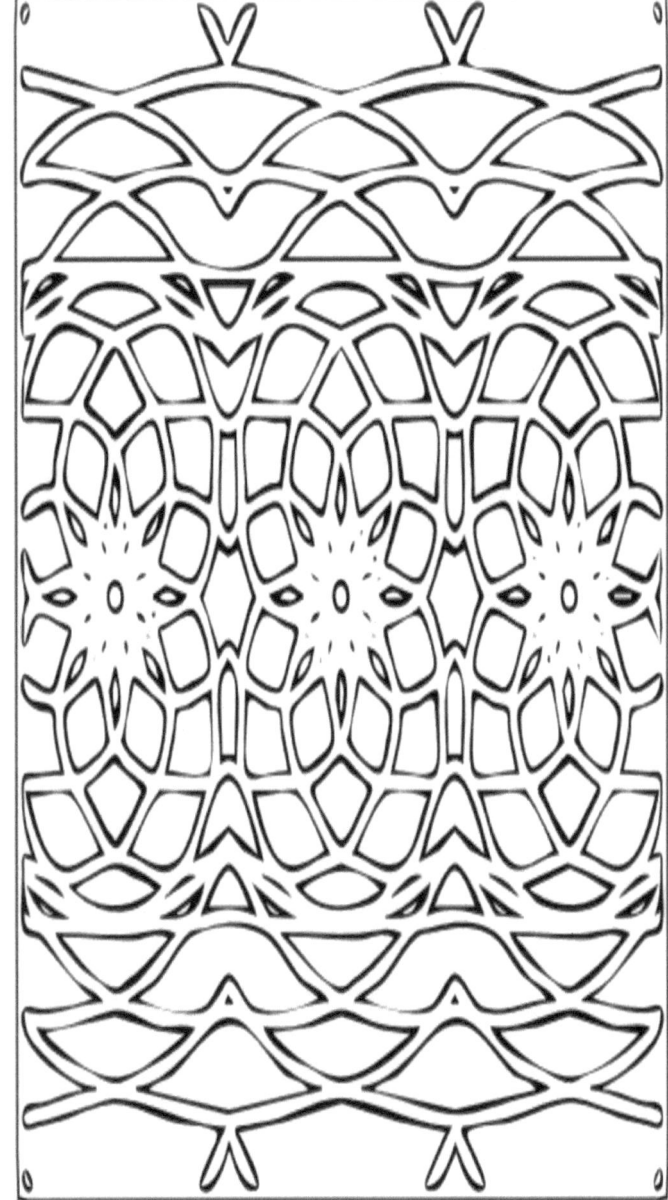

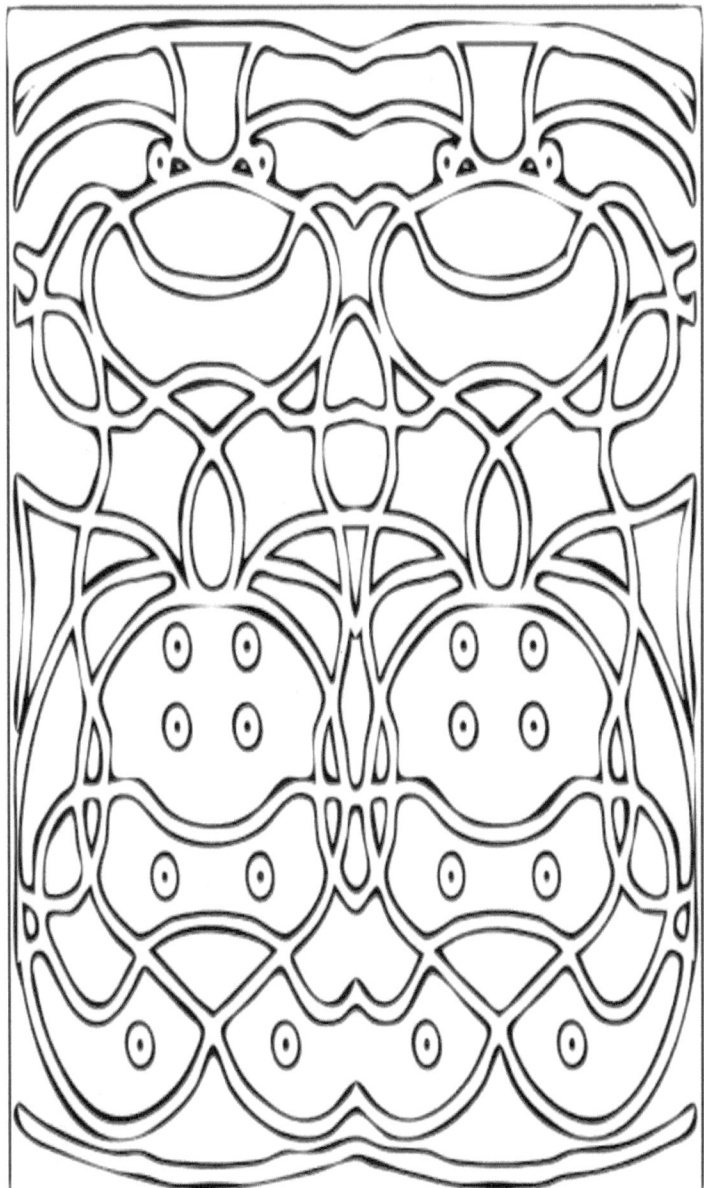

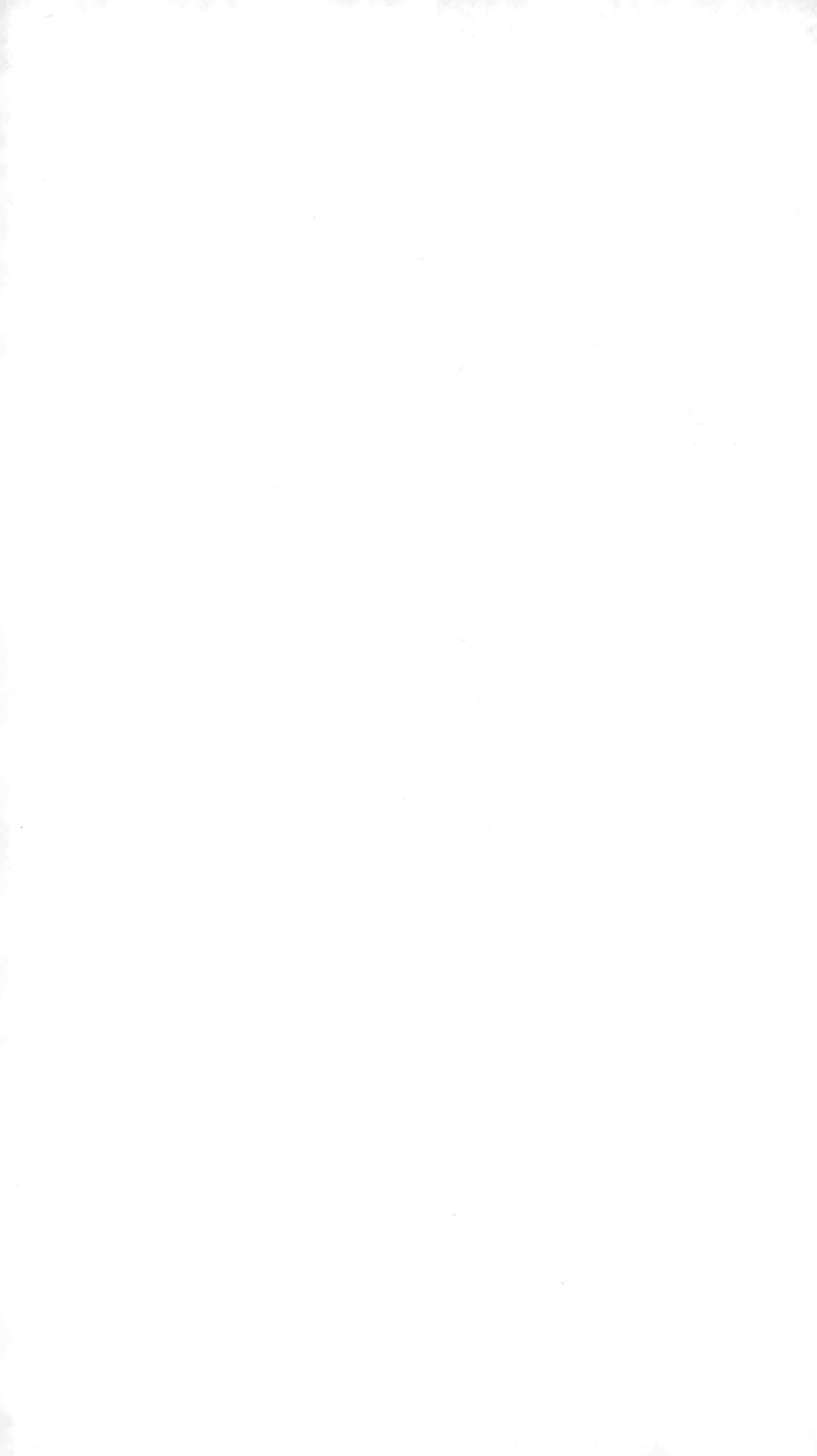

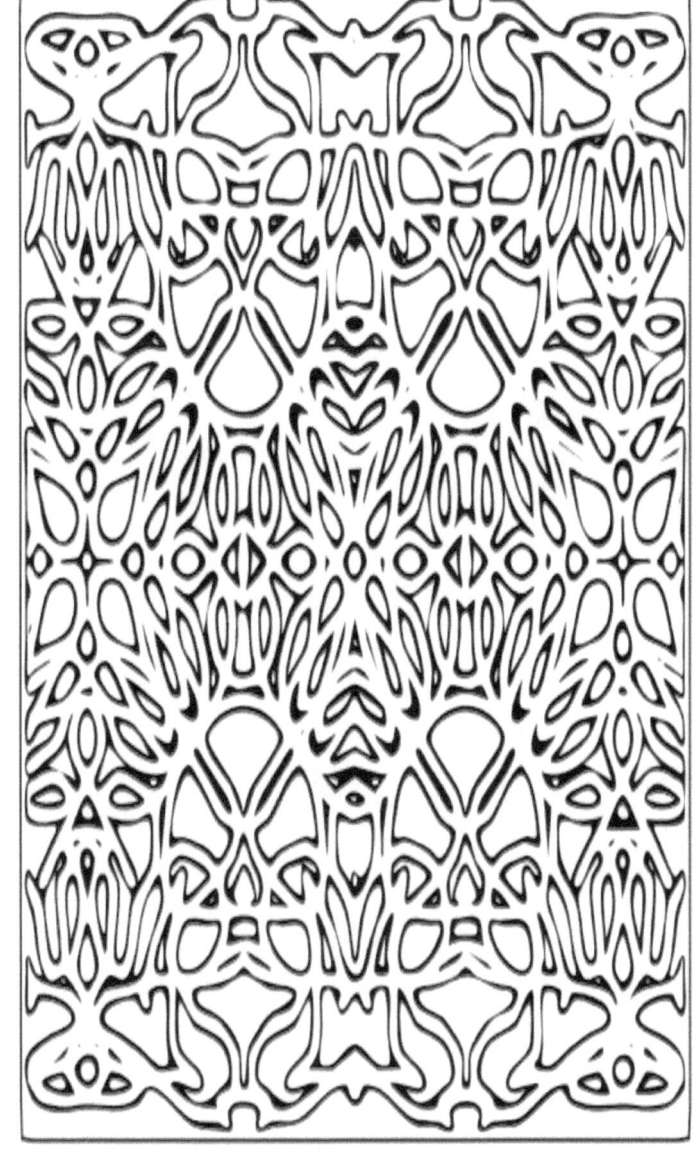

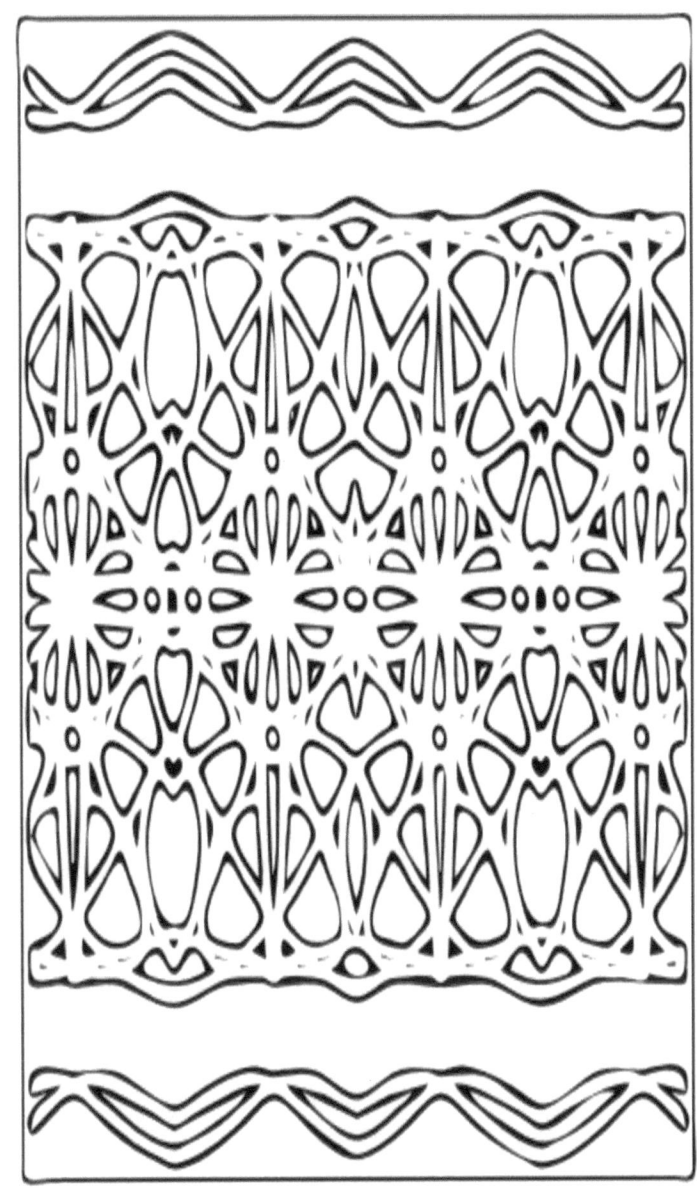

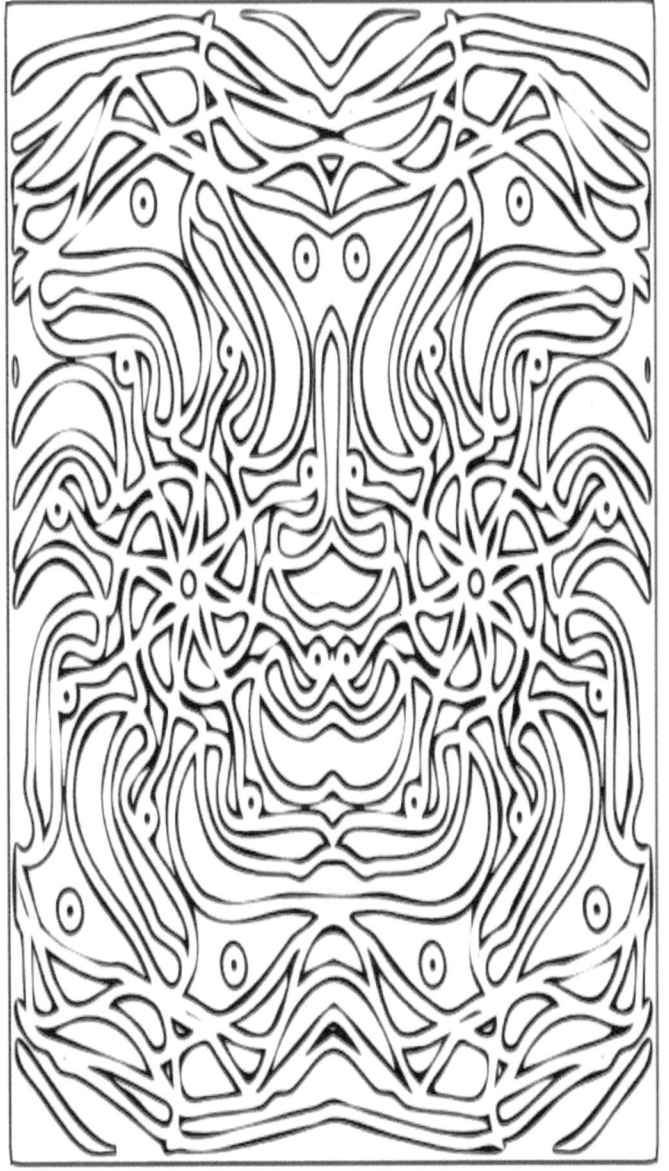

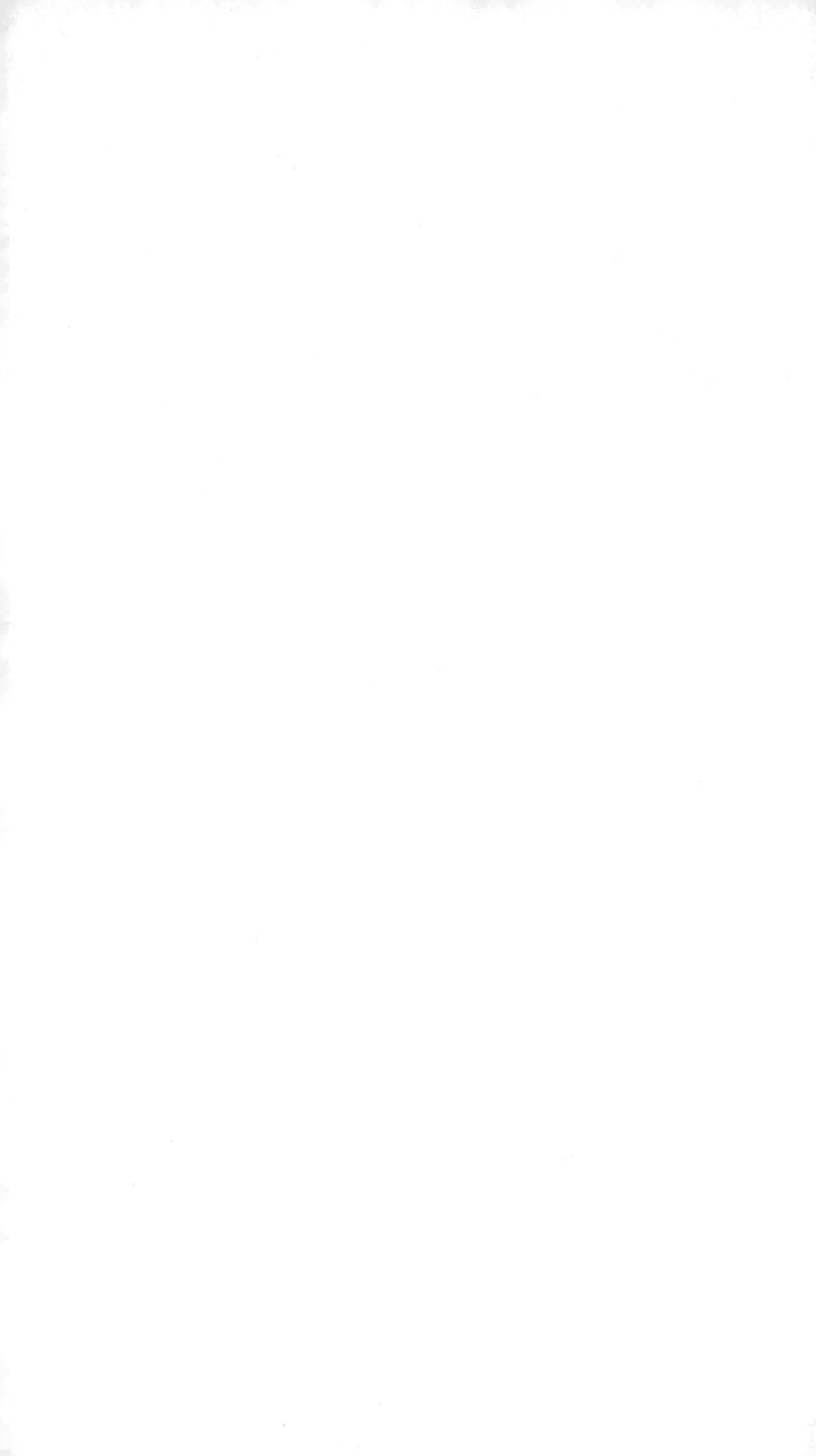

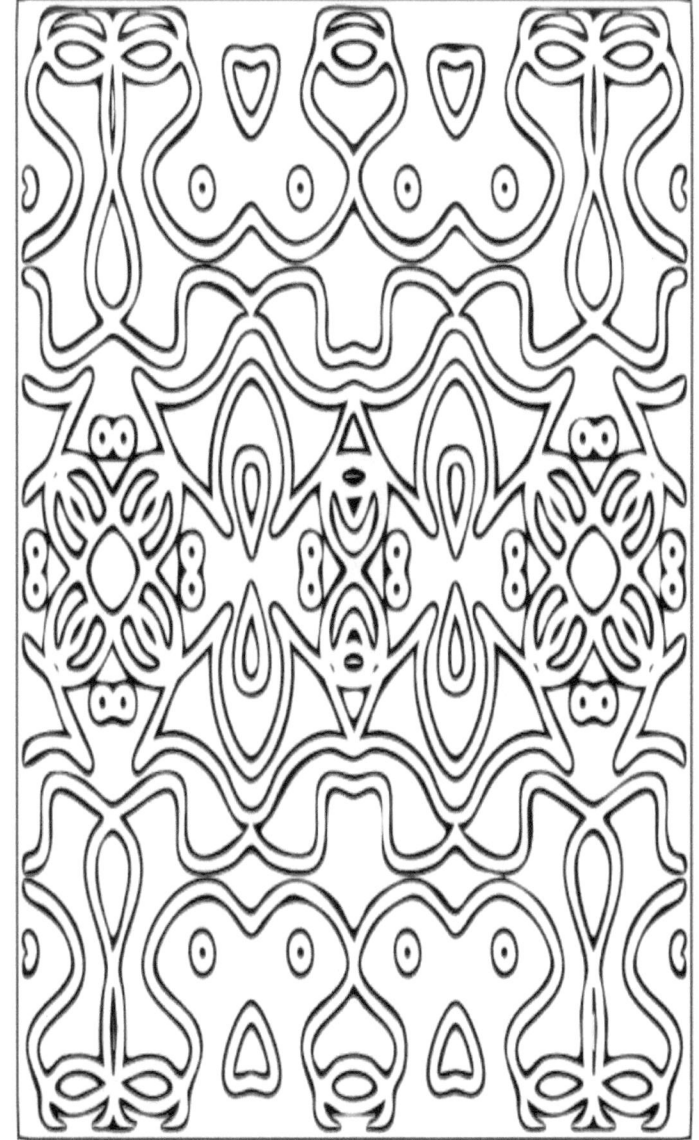

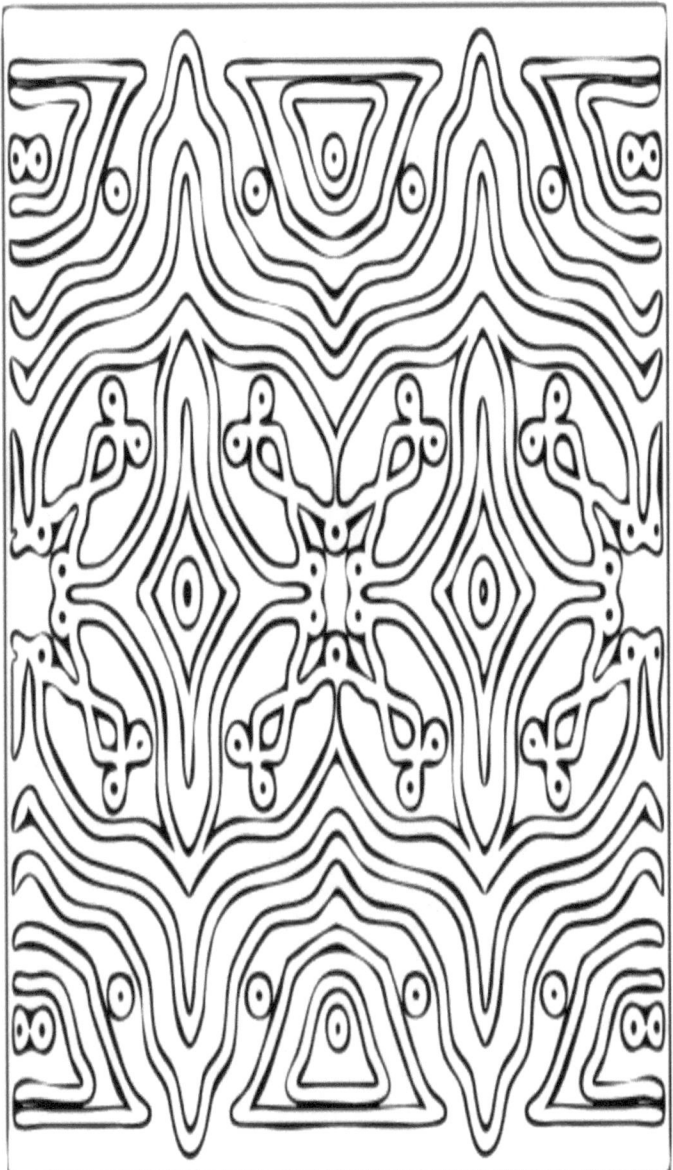

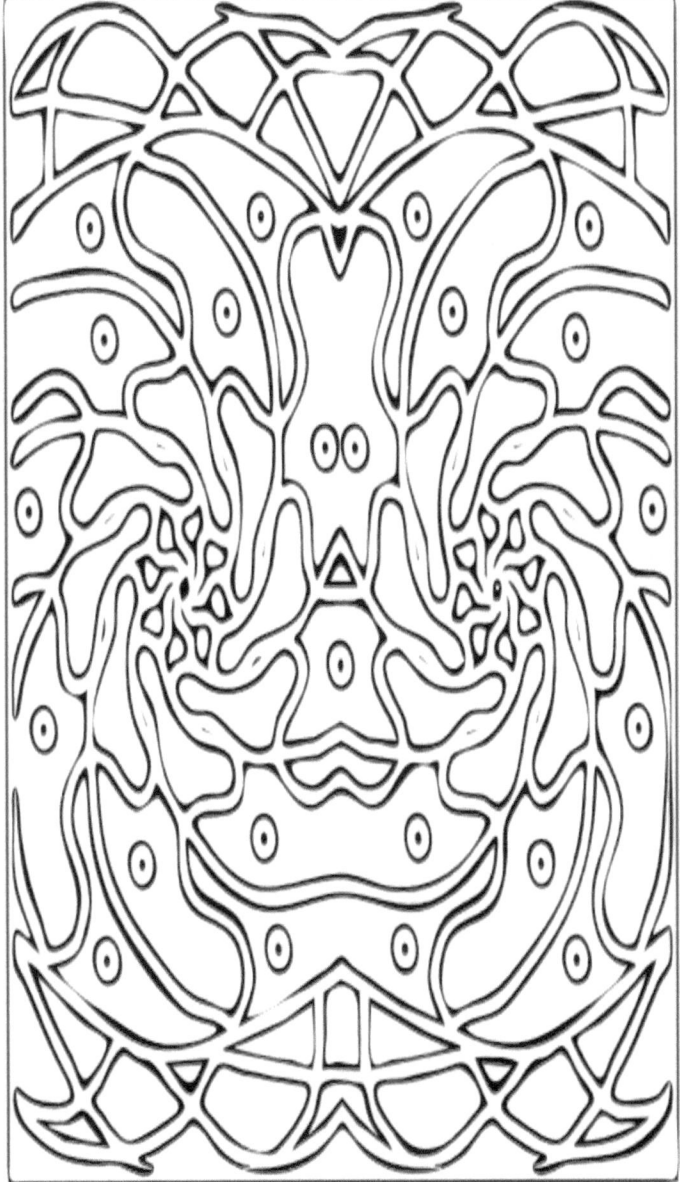

www.ingramcontent.com/pod-product-compliance
Lightning Source LLC
Chambersburg PA
CBHW021436170526
45164CB00001B/270